TALES FROM FIRST BASE

Related Titles from Potomac Books

*Baseball's Most Wanted™: The Top 10 Book
of the National Pastime's Outrageous Offenders,
Lucky Bounces, and Other Oddities*
—Floyd Conner

Pull Up a Chair: The Vin Scully Story
—Curt Smith

*You Never Forget Your First: Ballplayers Recall
Their Big League Debuts*
—Josh Lewin

TALES FROM FIRST BASE

The Best, Funniest, and Slickest First Basemen Ever

Brad Engel and Wayne Stewart

Potomac Books
Washington, D.C.

Library of Congress Cataloging-in-Publication Data
Engel, Brad, 1977–
    Tales from first base : the best, funniest, and slickest first basemen ever / Brad Engel and Wayne Stewart.
        p. cm.
    Includes bibliographical references and index.
    ISBN 978-1-59797-845-3 (hardcover : alk. paper)
    ISBN 978-1-59797-846-0 (electronic)
    1. Baseball players—United States—Anecdotes. 2. Base running (Baseball)—United States—Anecdotes. I. Stewart, Wayne, 1952– II. Title.
    GV863.A1E55 2013
    796.3570922–dc23
    [B]

                                                    2012045402

Printed in the United States of America on acid-free paper that meets the American National Standards Institute Z39-48 Standard.

Potomac Books
22841 Quicksilver Drive
Dulles, Virginia 20166

First Edition

10 9 8 7 6 5 4 3 2 1

To my family—wife Nancy, sons Scott and Sean, daughter-in-law Rachel, and grandson Nathan—and to all the wonderful and helpful people in my hometown of Donora, Pennsylvania.

—Wayne Stewart

To my wife Jill, son Carsen, parents Gerald and Elaine, brother Bryan, sister-in-law Jen, and nephews Drew, Ryan, and Evan, and to everyone who's ever offered me support and encouragement.

—Brad Engel

CONTENTS

INTRODUCTION

First base is a position that has produced many standouts, including more than a handful who have been inducted in baseball's Hall of Fame. It has also produced its share of funny, colorful characters; skillful sluggers; and defensive whizzes. All of these aspects of first base, including the socializing that goes on there, are covered in this book.

As a sort of ground rule for the book, we should note that many men in baseball play more than one position—aging outfielders, for instance, often find themselves switched to first base—so we consider a player to be a first baseman as long as he spent a considerable amount of time at that spot; if his tales are compelling, he will be mentioned in this book. It is a vague definition, but we will brook no squabbling. Men such as Stan Musial and Willie Stargell will be discussed in these pages.

Two other basic rules for this book: all statistics, records, and feats mentioned are current through the end of the 2012 season, unless otherwise noted; and players from the pre-1900 era, such as Cap Anson, are not included.

HUMOR

JOE PEPITONE
*New York Yankees 1962–1969; Houston Astros 1970; Chicago Cubs
1970–1973; Atlanta Braves 1973*

Joe "Pepi" Pepitone was a highly colorful first-sacker. He began his
major league career with the New York Yankees, a team that included
Mickey Mantle, Roger Maris (who was then one year removed from his
record-setting season in which he propelled 61 home runs to usurp Babe
Ruth as the home run king), and Whitey Ford.

Pepitone enjoyed a twelve-year career, hitting 219 lifetime home
runs. In his later seasons, during the hippie years, he was considered to
be among the first players to bring a metrosexual flair into the otherwise
macho world of the locker room. He was noted for using hair dryers,
hairpieces, and other tonsorial means of primping in the clubhouse.
Perhaps Pepitone had hair styling on the brain—when he became a
member of the Astros in 1970, the iconoclastic first baseman wryly
noted, "The Houston Astrodome is the biggest hairdryer in the world."

His Houston manager, old-school Harry "Harry the Hat" Walker,
must have been baffled by Pepitone. Perhaps that's why the first base-

man would spend only 75 games with Houston before finding himself traded to the Chicago Cubs.

Of course, joining the Cubs meant playing under another old-schooler, the acerbic Leo Durocher. In his book *Wrigleyville*, Peter Golenbock wrote that Pepitone was "an individualist," something the baseball establishment wasn't too fond of, and that he "was like a little kid in school who hated to be reprimanded or lectured by the principal. That Leo was the Cubs' principal made for a volatile relationship."

The first time Pepitone whipped out his hair dryer in the Cubs' locker room, it was so loud Durocher heard it from his office. When informed what the source of the din was, Durocher simply scratched his head and shut his door. A former teammate of Babe Ruth, Durocher found Pepitone's ways to be the antithesis of how a player should behave.

Pepitone ran up large bills, especially on clothes, and then expected the Cubs to bail him out. Once during a road trip he entered the club-house loaded down with four garment bags. Durocher stared in dismay, figuring Pepi had just enjoyed another wild shopping binge, until Pepitone grinned and assured him the bags were merely his laundry.

The free-spending Pepitone once commented, "I seldom refused autograph seekers, unless they were old enough to look like collection agents."

Even though he won three Gold Glove Awards—Chicago's second baseman Glenn Beckert called him the best defensive first-sacker he played alongside—it was said that Pepi disliked his pitchers firing the ball over to the bag on pickoff attempts. In his classic book *Ball Four*, former big league pitcher Jim Bouton wrote that when he was Pepitone's teammate on the Yankees, he observed Pepi mishandling a throw from third baseman Clete Boyer in the 1963 World Series, after Pepi lost sight of the ball camouflaged by the shirts of the spectators behind third base. After that, wrote Bouton, "he didn't want to handle the ball any-more than he had to."

During the 1964 World Series against the St. Louis Cardinals, speed merchant Lou Brock led off first, with Pepitone holding him on for Bouton. At that point Bouton signaled to his first baseman that a pickoff throw was forthcoming. To his amazement, Bouton saw

Pepitone "standing there shaking his head, tiny shakes because he didn't want anybody to see. It was the first time I ever saw anybody shake off a pickoff sign."

Several pitches later, just to rib Pepitone, Bouton again flashed the pickoff sign to see if he would once more shake off the play. Again, wanting no part of a throw, Pepitone, as if to say, "No. *Please* don't throw it my way," did indeed shake his pitcher off, just as a pitcher shakes off his catcher.

JOHN KRUK

San Diego Padres 1986–1989; Philadelphia Phillies 1990–1994; Chicago White Sox 1995

A very outspoken man, John Kruk was the type of person whose jokes were often at his own expense. After receiving notification via letter that he was accepted as a member of the 1991 All-Star squad, Kruk commented, "That's the first letter I got from [National League (NL) president] Bill White where I didn't have to pay a fine."

Two years later he had made the All-Star team again with the Phillies, and this time he would make humor history when he faced intimidating 6-foot-10 southpaw Randy Johnson. "The Big Unit" sent a 98-mile-per-hour fastball sailing over Kruk's head. Immediately, perhaps instinctively, Kruk reacted to the heart-stopping pitch by grabbing at his chest as if he needed a quick injection of epinephrine. After that brushback with death, he quickly went down on strikes, flailing away with futility and bailing out badly. In fact, even before the first offering from Johnson, Kruk was way off the plate, prompting writers to tease that he might as well have batted from the dugout. In short, his at bat versus Johnson is an All-Star memory that will live forever.

Kruk once observed, "I would think I drive most hitting coaches crazy. During one single at bat I used six different stances on six pitches. Oh yeah, I also struck out. So what do I know?"

On another occasion he joked, "Before the game they told me I looked like Babe Ruth. Then, in my [ugly] at bat against Don Carmen, I looked like Dr. Ruth."

After clean-living Dale Murphy joined Kruk on the Phillies, Kruk quipped, "We were twenty-four morons and a Mormon."

When Kruk opened a bar and named it "Third Base," he was asked how in the world he had come up with that name—after all, he had never played that position. He replied, "Because it's the last place you stop on the way home."

Kruk's physical appearance is far from glamorous, but that's the way he likes it—to him glamour is anathema. During his playing days he was listed as standing at 5-foot-10 and weighing in at around 204 pounds. Such a physique led pitcher Don Sutton to comment, "He looks like a guy who went to fantasy camp and decided to stay."

It should be noted that players' *listed* heights and weights are often inaccurate. A short man may want to be listed as being taller than he is while an overweight baseball player may shave off a pound or two so as not to be embarrassed when he sees his weight in print. In 1994 Kruk admitted that he had played in the previous season at 226 pounds. Observers claimed his weight was closer to 250. In any case, he began to diet and exercise during the off season, vowing to shed weight. As some of Kruk's pounds slipped away his manager, Jim Fregosi, seemed to be unconcerned that Kruk might shed too much weight and lose the sting in his bat. "I don't know if he can hit skinny," said Fregosi. "But if he has to, he can put on thirty pounds as quickly as anybody I've ever seen."

MARV THRONEBERRY

New York Yankees 1955–1959; Kansas City Athletics 1960; Baltimore Orioles 1961–1962; New York Mets 1962–1963

Only in New York. Only with the Mets. The New York Mets were born in 1962, and they suffered growing pains beyond belief. They were pathetic right out of the gate, dropping their first 9 games, and were mathematically eliminated from the pennant chase in early August. They managed to win exactly one-fourth of their decisions, going 40-120, disproving an old baseball saying that all teams win one-third of their games, lose one-third, and what they do with their remaining one-third will tell the tale of how good or how poor the club is. Their .250 win-loss percentage was the third worst of the modern era, and no team ever has dropped as many decisions in a single season as the "can't anybody here play this game?" Mets of 1962.

Few would argue that as poor a collection of players as this team was, comprising mostly castoffs and misfits, none more symbolized the laughable, ludicrous team than Marv "Marvelous Marv" Throneberry.

An oddity that typified the play of both the Mets in general and Throneberry in particular took place on June 17 of the Mets' inaugural season. According to one eyewitness, Throneberry came to the plate with two teammates aboard, Gene Woodling leading off second and Frank Thomas edging off first base. Throneberry hit a gap shot and lumbered around the bags for a triple in right-center. In true Mets style, when Throneberry rounded first, he missed the base. The umpire at third called him safe, but the Cubs appealed at second, not first, and the ump there called him out.

Mets manager Casey Stengel was apoplectic as he argued the call. Solly Hemus, then a Mets coach, stated that one run was permitted to score, and that one of the umpires working the bases had informed Stengel, "If you don't get out of here and they throw to first base [for an appeal there], you're not going to get any runs at all. He missed first *and* second."

As with much baseball lore, there are several versions of this story. One has it that a Mets coach placated "the Old Professor," telling him, "Don't bother arguing, Casey. He missed first base, too." Another version claims it was umpire Dusty Boggess who ruled Throneberry was out for missing *first*, but affirms that he had also missed second base.

One source states that when Stengel was told his man had missed both first and second, he blurted to his third base coach, "I know damn well he didn't miss third, he's standing on it."

As an aftermath to the play, sportswriter Jack Lang commented, "How could he be expected to remember where the bases were? He gets on so infrequently."

It's little wonder another famous writer, Jimmy Breslin, observed, "Having Marv Throneberry play for your team is like having Willie Sutton [notorious bank robber] work for your bank."

Even when the Mets emerged as a winning team, the 1962 episode was not forgotten. Sportswriter Leonard Koppett made a reference to it in his reporting: "Fifteen minutes after the Mets clinched their [1969] championship, their followers had torn up the Shea Stadium surface. . . . And, being true Mets fans with their roots in 1962, they missed first base."

Throneberry's performance encapsulated the Mets' futility. In 1962 he did hit 16 homers but managed only a .244 batting average and drove in just 49 runs over 116 contests. Plus, he somehow committed a whopping 17 errors at first base in just 97 games there.

Cleary a terrible man with the leather, Throneberry teased teammate Frank Thomas, who had just made two errors on a play, "What are you trying to do, take my fans away from me?"

On July 30, 1962, not long after Throneberry's debacle of missing two bases, the team celebrated Stengel's birthday. Throneberry asked why they hadn't done the same for him. "Why no cake?" he mused aloud. Stengel answered, "We was going to get you a birthday cake, but we figured you'd drop it."

JACK CLARK

San Francisco Giants 1975–1984; St. Louis Cardinals 1985–1987; New York Yankees 1988; San Diego Padres 1989–1990; Boston Red Sox 1991–1992

Jack Clark played first base and outfield, but not too well. An anonymous fan quipped after learning that Clark was reported to have been "born again," "Why is it Jack Clark can find God but not the cutoff man?" Sportswriter Lowell Cohn reported that on one play Clark "reacted to the ball with the speed of a sedated hippo."

Face it, Clark was better known for his offensive prowess and for what has to be his one biggest claim to fame—his homer to wrap up the 1985 National League Championship Series (NLCS) off Dodgers pitcher Tom Niedenfuer. "The only way that shot would have stayed in the ballpark," Niedenfuer grudgingly admired, "is if it hit the Goodyear blimp."

Quite appropriately, some observers called Clark "Jack the Ripper," as he did just that to the baseball—340 times for home runs, in fact. His high-water mark for homers was 35 in 1987, when he played for the Cardinals and came in third in the voting for the MVP Award after leading the NL in slugging and on-base plus slugging (1.055). However, he was also feared enough and patient enough to lead his league in walks drawn three times and on-base percentage once.

DICK STUART
*Pittsburgh Pirates 1958–1962; Boston Red Sox 1963–1964;
Philadelphia Phillies 1965; New York Mets 1966; Los Angeles Dodgers
1966; California Angels 1969*

Dick Stuart was a powerful first baseman who crushed 66 home runs in a single season (1956) while playing for Lincoln (Nebraska) in Class A ball in the minors. The following season, as he moved up the minor league ladder, he drilled 45 additional home runs in three different leagues.

By 1958 he made it to the big leagues with the Pirates, and he continued to display punch—he hit 16 homers in just 67 games that year, upped his total to 27 in 1959, and became a key part of the 1960 World Champion Pittsburgh Pirates (23 HR with 83 RBI).

His top home run outputs came in 1961 when he blasted 35, and in 1963, his first year in the AL after being swapped to the Boston Red Sox for catcher Jim Pagliaroni and pitcher Don Schwall, he came through with 42 homers (second in the AL to Harmon Killebrew), 319 total bases (best in the league), and 118 runs driven in—also good enough to top the league. Before Stuart, no player had ever hit 30 or more home runs with 100 or more RBI in both leagues.

Quite the character, Stuart once mused, "I want to walk down the street and hear them say, 'Jesus, there goes Dick Stuart!' I crave publicity." Another time, after he had been hit by a pitch on his batting helmet, he was asked if he felt dizzy. He replied, "No more than usual."

The 6-foot-4 Stuart was also a notoriously poor fielder, possessing about as much range as a flagpole sitter. Once, during a blustery game, a stray hot dog wrapper blew onto the field. Stuart made a stab at it and caught the paper cleanly. The fans, well aware of his propensity to boot such plays, responded with applause. Later Stuart would recount, "Errors are a part of my image. One night in Pittsburgh, thirty thousand fans gave me a standing ovation when I caught a hot dog wrapper on the fly." Earlier in his career spectators cheered him when he caught a bounding bat that had slipped out of the hands of a hitter.

At least Stuart was as candid as he was brutal with the glove. Errors were indeed a big part of the Stuart package. For seven straight seasons, from 1958 through 1964, he led the league in that category, and for him turning this rare trick was surprisingly easy—in 1958 he managed to lead the way with 16 errors, even though he played in only 67 games, much less than one half of the season. As a matter of fact, over his ten-year career, 1965 was the *only* full season in which he did not lead his league in misplays.

In 1963, he committed an ungodly 29 errors at first base, a position where great gloves make just a handful of errors—Stuffy McInnis made just one error in 1921 and Steve Garvey set a record with no errors in 1984. Stuart followed up that folly the next year with 24 more, the fourth and final (thank goodness) time he had 20 or more errors in a single season—and that's only because he ran out of time. He played only one more full season after 1964 and it wasn't with Boston (he was traded for Dennis Bennett, who would go on to win only 12 games with the Sox). Stuart had hit 75 homers during his stint with Boston and led the league in RBI once for them, but the front office had had it with his strikeouts and errors. After all, during Stuart's two seasons there he had committed 53 errors, in every way imaginable.

One newspaperman opined, "He's a Williams type player. He bats like Ted and fields like Esther." Writers quickly dubbed him Dr. Strangeglove, a name teammates naturally picked up—although Mickey Mantle said the Yankees called him Steel Fingers—and Stuart didn't seem to mind. "I know I'm the world's worst fielder," he stated, "but who gets paid for fielding? There isn't a great fielder in baseball getting paid the kind of dough I get for hitting." Former teammate Dick Groat summed up Stuart's situation as follows: "Dick's biggest problem was his lack of concentration—thinking about hitting instead of playing defense."

DICK ALLEN

Philadelphia Phillies 1963–1969, 1975–1976; St. Louis Cardinals 1970; Los Angeles Dodgers 1971; Chicago White Sox 1972–1974; Oakland Athletics 1977

Stuart didn't always receive standing ovations; he frequently heard his share of boo-birds after muffing a play. Fellow slugger Dick (a.k.a. Richie) Allen also experienced his share of catcalls, especially when he played in the City of Brotherly Love—better known in baseball circles as Philadelphia, the venue with a reputation so tough it was said that fans there would boo Santa Claus.

Allen, who made what was then considered to be good money, was a graduate of a high school in Wampum, Pennsylvania. Still, earning a hefty salary didn't guarantee happiness. He once stated, "I wish they'd shut the gates, and let us play ball with no press and no fans." He also said that while making a ton of money was fine, "the only thing I like about money is that it brings a grin to Mom's face. It's not that she cares so much about it, it's just that she thought I would wind up busted."

Unlike Stuart, Allen, the NL 1964 Rookie of the Year (when he led the league in total bases with 352) took heat not for his glove work, but for the perception that he was surly and that he didn't always play hard. However, his offensive numbers spoke for themselves. Using an unbelievably heavy bat of around 42 ounces (as a comparison, Mark McGwire typically used bats in the 32-ounce neighborhood), Allen compiled 351 lifetime homers to go with his 1,119 RBI and his career batting average of .292. As Jim Bouton once put it, in baseball different rules apply to superstars as opposed to ordinary players. "I mean, what's the good of a .220 hitter who obeys the curfew? Richie Allen doesn't obey the rules, hits 35 home runs, and knocks in over 100. I'll take him."

Still, such productivity wasn't enough to placate Philly fans. Allen found that the atmosphere there became so oppressive he decided to send a message to disgruntled spectators. Lacking a public address system and a megaphone, he used his cleats to carve out messages about as subtle as a lobotomy, boldly scrawling the word "BOO" into the dirt around the first base bag.

In fact, over a six-day period in 1969 he wrote many such barbed messages in the basic form, though not content, of an old song, "Love Letters in the Sand." Allen was, in effect, his own fan message board, albeit on a smaller scale than a ballpark scoreboard's Fan-O-Gram. Resenting authority figures, he "printed" the word "MOM" as a way of saying only his mother could tell him what to do and how to act.

Commissioner Bowie Kuhn informed Allen that he was to stop his antics, so the next time Allen took to the field he scribbled a response: "WHY?" During another game, according to Allen, a team official called down from his office to the dugout, ordering him to quit writing. Minutes later Allen left the bench, trotted to his position, and promptly inscribed a concise reply: "NO." Desperate to leave the Phillies, Allen used his rebellious behavior as leverage to force a trade and once wrote "OCTOBER 2," signifying the last day of the season, to indicate what he hoped would be (and what proved to be) his personal Independence Day.

After being a member of the Phillies from late in 1963 through 1969, he got his wish. The Cardinals took him in a blockbuster trade. The transaction was not only enormous, involving seven players, it was historic. Curt Flood, one of the principals in the trade, slated to go to the Phillies, refused to report to his new team, questioning the firmly established reserve clause in baseball. His actions would eventually pave the way for more players' rights, including their ability to gain mobility via free agency.

Early in the 1970 season, when reporters asked Allen what position he wanted to play for the Cardinals, he replied, "I'll play first, third, and left. I'll play anywhere—except Philadelphia." Ironically, he would return to Philadelphia, playing for the Phillies for a season and a half, in 1975.

The Cards kept him for just one season before dumping him, swapping him to the Los Angeles Dodgers for Ted Sizemore and Bob Stinson. The Dodgers also shipped him off after a single season, acquiring Tommy John from the Chicago White Sox in return. Thus, from 1969 through 1972 Allen played for four teams over four seasons.

In 1972, in his first year as a member of the Sox, Allen earned the MVP Award, based largely on his league-leading 37 home runs and 113 RBI, and on his .308 batting average, third best in the AL. He had found a home in Chicago, playing for a manager, Chuck Tanner, who appreciated him and didn't try to rein him in. Needless to say, Allen didn't hear too many boos from home fans that season.

Being traded so often soured Allen. Near the end of his career he said, "I once loved this game, but after being traded four times, I realize that it's nothing but a business. I treat my horses better than the owners treat us. It's a shame they've destroyed my love for the game."

Allen did, in fact, love and own horses, which led to another of his famous observations. In 1970 he was asked his opinion on artificial turf. He replied, "If a horse can't eat it, I don't want to play on it."

A reporter asked one of his managers, Gene Mauch, if a slumping Allen was having difficulty with the high fastball. "No," Mauch replied, "the fast highball." Another time Mauch was asked how he handled his star player. He confessed his only strategy was "play him, fine him, and play him again."

MARK GRACE
Chicago Cubs 1988–2000; Arizona Diamondbacks 2001–2003

When slick-fielding Mark Grace was with the Chicago Cubs he once performed a sort of baseball calligraphy act. Right smack-dab in the middle of a game in 1997, Grace and counterpart Larry Walker of the Colorado Rockies delivered messages in the dirt to each other. The two friends treated the Coors Field crowd to some old-fashioned fun at the ballpark.

As Mike Kiley recounted in the *Chicago Sun-Times*, Grace wrote with his finger, "You Can't Hit .400." Upon his return to defense Walker honestly replied, "I Know." The exchange continued when Walker spelled out "You Can't Hit .300," deliberately following a Grace ground-out to Walker. By that point in his career Grace had already hit .300 six times, and he would retire with a lifetime .303 batting average—obviously, Walker was just giving Grace the business.

Walker altered the intent of the game by dabbling in the dirt that he was going to bunt. He wasn't so prophetic, though. The back-and-forth with Grace ended after Walker instead struck out for the third time, prompting Grace to pen, "Hat Trick."

There were even some things said in the sand that couldn't be printed the next day, but the *Sun-Times* did offer this: "'He started it,' Grace said afterward. 'We've been friends since A-ball. We're always jabbering back and forth at each other, but this is the first time we've played him where he's played first base.'"

Grace, like any ballplayer positioned near the stands, has heard some hecklers over the years, but he handled them with ease, remaining unruffled. "I've had guys yell, 'I was with your sister last night.' I know that's not true—I don't have a sister."

Even when dealing with an opponent who cheated, Grace stayed cool. He commented on a young pitcher who had been caught loading up on a pitch versus Grace's team: "You have to give him credit. Most guys don't start cheating until later in their career."

When Grace wasn't busy filling Kiley's notebook with tomfoolery like his antics with Walker, Grace was, well, filling Kiley's notebook with one-liners. In late February 1999, at the Cubs' spring-training facility in Mesa, Arizona, Grace was in rare form.

His first day on the field at Fitch Park, Grace weighed in on the story of country music star Garth Brooks's tryout with the San Diego Padres. The affable first baseman said, "The difference between me and Garth Brooks is that I can't sing and he can't play baseball."

Grace, a throwback to the simpler times of baseball—when preparing for the long season merely meant showing up in time for spring training—rarely touched a weight during his sixteen-year career and enjoyed non-performance-enhancing drugs like alcohol and tobacco. "Watching [teammate] Rod Beck save 51 in a season will drive anyone to smoke," he said.

Of course Grace wasn't above looking for any edge he could gain. When batting in daytime games, in which he could observe the shadow of the opposing catcher, he would make it a point to note where the catcher was setting up—toward the outside part of the plate or the inner part. Such information helped him focus on where upcoming pitches would be headed.

Grace even collected more hits than any other big leaguer over the 1990s (1,754) while also leading the majors with 364 doubles. Furthermore, he did it in a manner that was a bit unorthodox for that time period—unlike the vast majority of hitters, Grace rarely used batting gloves, save for very cold days.

ERNIE BANKS
Chicago Cubs 1953–1971

While Grace was one of the most popular Cubs players ever, most fans agree that *the* favorite Cub of all time is Ernie Banks—after all, he didn't get the nickname "Mr. Cub" for nothing.

Unfortunately for Cubs fans, there were some years in which Banks was the only bright spot in the club; he seemingly carried the team. That led former manager and player Jimmy Dykes to comment, "Without Ernie Banks, the Cubs would finish in Albuquerque."

While Banks is most famous for his upbeat words, like "It's a great day for a ballgame. Let's play two," and for his reference to his home ballpark as "beautiful Wrigley Field," he has also come up with a few other gems.

Once he joked that his "ultimate dream is to have my own bank, maybe in Paris. I'd call it Banks's Bank on the Left Bank."

Another first-sacker, Mike Hargrove, once noted, "I never knew anybody who said they like doubleheaders except Ernie Banks, and I think he was lying."

Banks's manager, Leo Durocher, joked that his star first baseman (Banks also excelled early on as a shortstop) "never remembered a sign or forgot a newspaperman's name."

However, it was patently clear that Banks was adored in Chicago and knew how to project his ever present optimism. Teammate Fergie Jenkins concluded, "I don't think these people at Wrigley Field ever saw but two players they liked—Billy Williams and Ernie Banks. Billy never said anything, and Ernie always said the right thing."

BILL BUCKNER

Los Angeles Dodgers 1969–1976; Chicago Cubs 1977–1984;
Boston Red Sox 1984–1987, 1990; California Angels 1987–1988;
Kansas City Royals 1988–1989

Yes, Bill Buckner's name is most associated with the routine ground ball that scooted between his legs in the sixth game of the 1986 World Series, but there's much more to the man than that fiasco.

As far as accomplishments go, he was an All-Star in 1981, one of two seasons he led his league in doubles. He was steady and durable, hitting .289 lifetime over a twenty-two-year career. He also led the NL in hitting (.324 in 1980). On the debit side, he once committed 17 errors at first base in just 105 games while playing for the 1981 Cubs.

Buckner has maintained his dignity despite the ignominy that went with his costly misplay when he was with the Boston Red Sox in the World Series. He philosophically stated, "I can't remember the last time I missed a ground ball. I'll remember that one."

Some of the teasing that goes on in baseball qualifies as gallows humor. Onetime Kansas City Royals manager Billy Gardner teased, "I heard that Billy Buckner tried to commit suicide over the winter. He stepped in front of a car, but it went through his legs."

Like many ballplayers, Buckner wasn't immune to superstition. Lenny Randle once said, "Bill Buckner had a 19-game hitting streak going and always wore the same underwear. Of course, he didn't have any friends."

PETE ROSE

Cincinnati Reds 1963–1978, 1984–1986; Philadelphia Phillies 1979–
1983; Montreal Expos 1984

In a perfect world the phrases "all-time hits leader" and "banned from baseball for life" shouldn't go together. But in the real world they do. The driven, almost monomaniacal Pete Rose eclipsed Ty Cobb as the man with the most career hits, breezing by Cobb's total of 4,191, as a member of the Cincinnati Reds, and not coming to a halt until he owned 4,256 base hits. In 1984 when his second wife, Carol, gave birth to a boy, Pete's second son, he wanted to name him Tyrus, as in Tyrus Raymond Cobb, but he had to settle with the name Tyler in a compromise with Carol.

An ex-teammate of Rose, Merv Rettenmund, was well aware of Pete's focus.

> He was special inasmuch as the intensity he brought per at bat.
> We're talking about believing in yourself. Thousands of players,
> I believe, that came up the road had more ability than Pete, but
> he had 5,000 hits [hyperbole—he actually had 4,256], and he
> never gave an at bat away.

Rose broke many other records, including setting all-time highs for games played, plate appearances, and at bats. A more obscure record is his mark for having played in more winning games (1,972) than any other big leaguer. He told *Time* magazine that that total represents more games than Joe DiMaggio played in, and that it would take someone nineteen consecutive seasons of playing for a team that won 100 games during each of those years just to come close to his total.

Furthermore, Rose was so versatile he could play virtually any position on the diamond—he won the NL Rookie of the Year Award as a second baseman and went on to play at every defensive spot except shortstop, pitcher, and catcher. For the purposes of this book, if a man played first for any length of time, he was a first baseman. Plus, in Rose's case, if you break the outfield into its three positions, Rose actually played first base more than any other position. He was at first for 939 games; the next highest total for him was 673 games in left field.

While most fans don't associate Rose with defense, he was actually the highest-ranked fielder at four defensive spots, leading the National League in fielding percentage in 1970 as a right fielder when he committed just one error; in 1974, while playing left field, again misplaying the ball only once; two years later, while stationed at third base; and once more in 1980, as a first baseman. In fact, in three of those seasons his fielding percentage was the same, at a sterling .997.

One thing every fan thinks of when the subject of Rose comes up is his hustle, hence his nickname "Charlie Hustle." There was no such thing as a walk for Rose. After drawing ball four, he would sprint to first base like a paperboy being chased by a pit bull. He joked about his aggressive style of play, "I think it's smarter to slide head first. I'd rather have an arm spiked than an ankle—plus you get your picture in the paper."

Rose absolutely loved to win. Even in an exhibition game such as the 1979 All-Star Game he dashed around third and barreled into catcher Ray Fosse with the force of a blitzing panzer tank, hell-bent on ending the game with a resounding crash. At the time he justified his actions by saying, "I just want to get to that plate as quickly as I can. Besides, nobody told me they changed it to girls' softball between third and home." Some critics carped about the game-winning play, but it was the *only* way Rose knew to play. As he put it, "Somebody's got to win and somebody's got to lose—and I believe in letting the other guy lose."

Rose was very capable of trading verbal jabs with other players. When he was with the Reds he glanced over at teammate Wayne Granger, a 6-foot-2 pitcher who was around 160 pounds, and quipped, "He's so skinny the only place he could have won a college letter was Indiana." Another time he razzed longtime teammate Tony Perez, "How can anyone as slow as you pull a muscle?"

He also got off a good one at the expense of one of his managers, Sparky Anderson. He told Sparky, "I played a more important part in your life than your mother. She only carried you for nine months, I carried you for nine years."

The media was a target for Rose, too. He once told a collected group of sportswriters, "I go to the park sick as a dog, and when I see my uniform hanging there, I get well right away. Then I see some of you guys, and I get sick again."

At times Rose sounded almost like a comedian delivering one-liners. When he was forty-four years old he joked, "Doctors tell me I have the body of a thirty-year-old. I know I have the brain of a fifteen-year-old. If you've got both, you can play baseball." He also noted of Philadelphia Phillies fans, "Some of these people would boo the crack in the Liberty Bell."

He joked frequently about his wealth. "I wish there was some way I could have gotten a college education," he began, and then added the punch line: "I'm thinking about buying a college, though." On another occasion he quipped, "With the money I'm making, I should be playing two positions." Then there was his reply to a writer who asked Rose, then in his forties, if he still enjoyed the game of baseball. Rose grinned and said, "Sure I do, and if someone paid you $6,000 a game, you'd have fun as well."

Sometimes Rose was funny even when he didn't intend to be. When he was asked for his opinion about interleague play, he said he felt that "it would take some of the lust off the All-Star Game."

As good as Rose was, his style of hitting didn't please powerful Mickey Mantle, prompting him to say, "If I had played my career hitting singles like Pete Rose, I'd wear a dress."

Rose was on the receiving end of a Jay Leno joke when he served a five-month prison term in 1990 for two felony counts of filing false income tax returns. The late-night comedian asked, "If Pete Rose bets on prison softball games, will he be barred from jail for life?"

Even his ex-wife, Karolyn Rose, took a verbal slap at him when she stated, in 1979, "You have to give Pete credit for what he's accomplished. He never went to college and the only book he ever read was *The Pete Rose Story*."

WILLIE STARGELL
Pittsburgh Pirates 1962–1982

Willie Stargell played more games in left field (1,229) than at first, but he did man the first base position for 848 contests.

It was Stargell who, as the Pittsburgh Pirates' clubhouse elder statesman, led the 1979 squad to the World Championship, breezing by the Reds in a 3–0 sweep of the NLCS, then outlasting the tough Baltimore Orioles in seven contests. Stargell earned the nickname "Pops" from the young teammates whom he took under his protective, powerful wings, not unlike a mother hen.

Stargell's wit was almost, but not quite, as impressive as his power. Once, when a writer told Stargell that Pirates teammate Dave Parker had named him as his idol, Stargell observed with a grin, "That's pretty good, considering that Dave's previous idol was himself."

Stargell was also quick with his humor the time he was running off first base on the pitch—presumably on a botched hit-and-run play—and the catcher fired a strike to second that beat Stargell by two country miles. Realizing he was about to be called dead *prior* to arrival at the bag, he stopped short, looked up at the umpire, and signaled "time out" with his hands.

A standout hitter—1,540 RBI and a .282 batting average over twenty-one seasons—he could afford to joke about his occasional failures. "If I'm hitting, I can hit anyone. If not, my twelve-year-old son can get me out." When it came to facing the best in the game, Stargell said of southpaw sensation Sandy Koufax, "Trying to hit him was like trying to drink coffee with a fork." Years later, when Stargell was asked what his greatest thrill in baseball had been, he came back with this: "When Sandy Koufax retired."

Stargell wasn't too keen on facing knuckleball artists like Phil Niekro, either. The knuckler, he said, was "like a butterfly with hiccups. If you don't have a long fly swatter, you're in trouble."

Stargell could be philosophical, too. He once said, "When they start the game, they don't yell, 'Work ball.' They say, 'Play ball.'" He also observed, "They give you a round bat and they throw you a round ball. And then they tell you to hit it square." Another time he stated, "I'm always amazed when a pitcher becomes angry at a hitter for hitting a home run off him. When I strike out, I don't get angry at the pitcher, I get angry at myself."

ROD CAREW
Minnesota Twins 1967–1978; California Angels 1979–1985

The Panamanian seven-time batting champ was a joy to watch at the plate. Rod Carew, a lifetime .328 hitter, went from being the 1967 AL Rookie of the Year with the Twins to becoming an All-Star every season but his final one, 1985, and culminated it all by becoming a Hall of Famer in 1991 while somehow being left off 42 ballots.

When *The Sporting News* published a book called *Baseball's 100 Greatest Players*, they summarized Carew's performance as follows: "He handled the bat with the same efficiency Merlin coaxed from his wand. Rod Carew was a baseball magician with the power to make well-placed pitches disappear into every conceivable outfield gap."

Carew truly did handle the bat with the dexterity of a diamond cutter and could place the ball anywhere on a baseball diamond. "He could bunt .300 if he tried," longtime manager Billy Martin said.

Former Twins teammate Steve Brye added, "Rod Carew could get more hits with a soup bone than I could get with a rack full of bats. He can do anything he wants to up there." And former infielder Alan Bannister gushed, "He's the only guy I know who can go four for three."

Carew liked to flash his sense of humor. When asked his opinion of Mike Boddicker's stuff, Carew critiqued, "His pitches remind me of the garbage I take out at night."

DON BAYLOR

Baltimore Orioles 1970–1975; Oakland Athletics 1976, 1988; California Angels 1977–1982; New York Yankees 1983–1985; Boston Red Sox 1986–1987; Minnesota Twins 1987

Don Baylor was mainly an outfielder by trade, but he did spend some time at first base. He played under many managers and once commented, "Playing for Yogi [Berra] is like playing for your father. Playing for Billy [Martin] is like playing for your father-in-law."

Regardless of his manager, Baylor excelled. His finest season was in 1979, when he led the AL in runs scored, with 120; runs driven in, 139; and home runs, 36—all career bests. Surprisingly, that was the only season he was a member of an All-Star roster. As fearless as they come, he led his league for the most times hit by pitches—an eye-popping and body-aching eight times. Among players from the modern era, he still ranks second on the all-time hit by pitch list. He had, in fact, ranked first until Craig Biggio was hit twenty times more than Baylor's total of 267.

Baylor, who took many a shot in the ribs, once took a ribbing from one of his coaches with the Angels, Merv Rettenmund, who kidded, "He's the guts of the Angels, our triple threat: he can hit, run, and lob."

When Baylor became a manager, he turned the tables, poking fun at one of his players, "When we broke camp this spring, I fined [Bob] Shirley for making the club."

While he was still a player, Baylor had shown he had the right stuff to become a manager. Charles Zabransky, retired Yankees clubhouse attendant, recalled, "He was like God in the Yankees clubhouse. When you did wrong, he went in there and balled you out—you had to listen to him because he knew what he was talking about. He was like a cop, he took care of the guys."

ZEKE BONURA

Chicago White Sox 1934–1937; Washington Senators 1938, 1940;
New York Giants 1939; Chicago Cubs 1940

Born Henry Bonura, the man who came to be known as Zeke broke onto the major league scene with a resounding boom in 1934, driving home 110 runs for the Chicago White Sox. Prior to that season only five American League rookies had even compiled 100-plus RBI.

He was once asked why he seemed so depressed about being traded from the Washington Senators to the New York Giants in December 1938. He said, with a perfectly straight face, "Now I won't be able to sign my letters Senator Henry J. Bonura, Democrat, Louisiana."

NORM CASH

Chicago White Sox 1958–1959; Detroit Tigers 1960–1974

In 1961 Norm Cash of the Detroit Tigers won the AL batting crown when he hit a lusty .361, by far the best he would ever hit in the majors. As a matter of fact, the following season he plummeted to .243 and would never again hit higher than .283. Additionally, his single season 118-point drop-off was the deepest plunge ever for a returning batting champ. Later he looked back and, perhaps only somewhat jokingly, stated, "The only mistake I made in my whole baseball career was hitting .361 that one year, because ever since then people have expected me to keep on doing it."

Another mistake he made, though, was using corked bats, ones he operated on in a woodshop he had in his house. He confessed later that he had used the illegal bat in 1961 (and in subsequent seasons), when he swatted a career high 41 of his 377 lifetime roundtrippers. He would go on to quip about his baseball sin, "I owe my success to expansion pitching, a short right field fence, and my hollow bats."

Cash was not immune from striking out, doing so 1,091 times over his 6,705 big league at bats. He observed, "Pro-rated at 500 at bats a year, that means for two years out of the fourteen I played, I never even touched the ball."

Speaking of exercises in futility, one day Cash had to face the great Nolan Ryan and his untouchable stuff. Cash astonished the home plate umpire and virtually everyone else in the ballpark when he trudged to the plate lugging a leg from a clubhouse table instead of a bat—not exactly a corked bat, but illegal nevertheless. He explained, "I had as much chance with that as with a bat."

One of his funnier comments made him sound like a Don Rickles clone. "Baltimore," he said, "is a very exciting town—for excitement just before the game I went down the street and watched a hubcap rust."

ORLANDO CEPEDA

San Francisco Giants 1958–1966; St. Louis Cardinals 1966–1968; Atlanta Braves 1969–1972; Oakland Athletics 1972; Boston Red Sox 1973; Kansas City Royals 1974

The man who went by nicknames "Cha Cha" and "Baby Bull" wasn't well known for being a baseball raconteur, but he tells one story about spitball artist Gaylord Perry from their days together on the San Francisco Giants.

"Once he threw me a spitter at first base to pick off a runner. The ball sank a foot and I dropped it. When I threw it back to him it was still wet and sank again. The runners advanced a base and I got an error!"

In the 1970s, Orlando Cepeda wound up serving a five-year jail sentence for possession of and importing illegal drugs, and he had this to say about prison: "As a former baseball player, I find this not unlike minor league training camp—living together, eating together, and a bedtime curfew."

When it came to hitting, Cepeda was always serious. Like Dick Allen, Pete Rose, and Rod Carew, he also won the Rookie of the Year Award (1958) with the Giants as well as an MVP Award (1967) with the St. Louis Cardinals, and he won both awards unanimously, becoming the first National Leaguer to sweep all first-place votes for the MVP. A lifetime .297 hitter, he owns 379 career homers.

WILL CLARK

San Francisco Giants 1986–1993; Texas Rangers 1994–1998; Baltimore Orioles 1999–2000; St. Louis Cardinals 2000

The man with the poetic moniker "Will the Thrill" was a prolific hitter. Will Clark once led the NL in runs driven in when he had 109 ribbies in 1988 for the San Francisco Giants—that was one of four seasons he topped the century mark for RBI. He also hit over .300 for his career (.303) and was a six-time All-Star.

Like Cepeda, Clark doesn't have a slew of funny stories or quotes associated with his name. However, in 1989, when he was with the Giants and played in the World Series that was interrupted by a devastating earthquake, he remarked, "I knew something was wrong when the ground was moving faster than I was."

JIMMIE FOXX

Philadelphia Athletics 1925–1935; Boston Red Sox 1936–1942; Chicago Cubs 1942, 1944; Philadelphia Phillies 1945

One player who instilled fear with near-Ruthian impact had a nickname that reflected his strength and his intimidating ways. The man was James Emory Foxx (a.k.a. Double X), also known as the Beast. A bit of trivia: the character played by Tom Hanks in *A League of Their Own* was based on Foxx, who actually managed the All-American Girls Professional Baseball League.

In 1933, eight years after Foxx broke into the majors as a mere eighteen-year-old, he did something only Babe Ruth had done, and something no man has done since. He led the league in both strikeouts and in batting average. He hit .356 with the Philadelphia Athletics, en route to winning the Triple Crown, and whiffed 93 times, a modest total by today's standards, especially among power hitters. By way of contrast, in 2008 Arizona's Mark Reynolds set a new single season record for striking out an astronomical 204 times, then promptly went out and upped that to an embarrassing total of 223 the following season.

From the time he was twenty-one years old through the age of twenty-eight, Foxx cracked 327 homers, an average of 41 per season, and drove in 1,106 runs, close to 140 each year. It's hardly surprising, then, to learn that he was the first man to take home three MVP Awards, and he accomplished this in just one decade, the 1930s. He and Albert Pujols are the only first basemen to win three MVP trophies.

Further, on two occasions Foxx hit the ball so hard it sailed out of Chicago's Comiskey Park. Only two other men ever managed that feat, Babe Ruth and Hank Greenberg. Plus, only Ruth, Foxx, and Hack Wilson were able to hit 50-plus homers with 200 or more hits and 150-plus RBI in one season. In one respect Foxx outdid Ruth—and everyone else, for that matter. Of all the players who hit 500 or more homers, Foxx was the youngest man to reach the milestone at thirty-two years and 338 days.

With 534 homers over his twenty-year career (when he retired only Ruth owned more lifetime blasts) and more than 1,900 RBI, it's no wonder pitchers such as Lefty Gomez were in awe of the slugger. Gomez said that Foxx was so strong, "he has muscles in his hair." He also stated, "Jimmie Foxx wasn't scouted, he was trapped."

Another time when Gomez was on the mound facing Foxx, Gomez's catcher, fellow future Hall of Famer Bill Dickey, asked him what he wanted to throw to Foxx. Gomez snapped, "I don't want to throw him nothin'. Maybe he'll just get tired of waitin' and leave."

Gomez must have been almost obsessed with Foxx—he was still coming up with hyperbolic quotes about him decades after he last faced him in a contest. "When Neil Armstrong first set foot on the moon," Gomez once said, "he and all the space scientists were puzzled by an unidentifiable white object. I knew immediately what it was. That was a home run ball hit off me in 1937 by Jimmie Foxx."

Another great pitcher who knew what it was like to be stung by Foxx's power was Waite Hoyt. When Hoyt was in the last stage of his career, after a game he had just lost on a booming Foxx homer, he was asked by a young player, Sammy Byrd, what had happened to his once-stunning fastball. "Sonny," replied Hoyt, "you'll probably find it bouncing around upstairs at Shibe Park right now."

RON FAIRLY

Los Angeles Dodgers 1958–1969; Montreal Expos 1969–1974; St. Louis Cardinals 1975–1976; Oakland Athletics 1976; Toronto Blue Jays 1977; California Angels 1978

A reliable ballplayer, Ron Fairly went on to become an entertaining broadcaster. Once in a while he'd stumble, but his missteps on the air endeared him to many and induced much laughter.

One of his best quotes, which caused his listeners to scratch their heads, was, "He fakes a bluff." Another one was, "Last night I neglected to mention something that bears repeating." Then there was the time he said, "Bruce Sutter has been around for a while and he's pretty old. He's thirty-five years old, that will give you some idea how old he is."

He also described a play on the air thus: "That's another example of the lack of speed the Giants have—or don't have." After witnessing a Mike Schmidt homer, Fairly quipped, "I hit one that far once and I still bogeyed the hole."

Fairly was also capable of painting a colorful word picture. He spoke of Angels first baseman Wally Joyner as "such a good, All-American kid. You want to stand next to him in a rainstorm because you know lightning won't hit him."

During Fairly's waning years as a player he was asked why he didn't appear to be losing his speed. His quick comeback was, "There was nothing to lose."

BILL TERRY
New York Giants 1923–1936

The last right-hander, and the last National Leaguer, to hit .400 or better (.401 in 1930) was Bill Terry. Known as Memphis Bill, he had great
moments as a player and as a manager. He won three pennants, two as
a player-manager for the New York Giants (in 1933 and 1936) and
another when he served exclusively as a manager in 1937, and he also
won a World Championship in 1933. Best known for his hitting, Terry
was able to lead his league in assists 5 times.

He said of his magnificent 1930 campaign, "To hit .400 you need
a great start and you can't have a slump. The year I did it, I was around
.410, .412 all season and I was really hitting the ball on the nose. Hitting
is a business. With two strikes, you really protect that plate." His 254
hits that year stood for decades as the second most ever for a single season, and is still the most in NL play, tied with Lefty O'Doul's. A lifetime
.341 hitter, Terry was clearly one of the greatest hitters ever, but his .401
is a bit tainted in one respect. The 1930 season was known as the Year
of the Rabbit Ball, and juiced-up baseballs soared all over and out of
parks across the land.

That season, a boom year as freakish as a carnival sideshow, featured
the entire National League hitting .303, an all-time record, and scoring
more runs than ever before. Perhaps just as stunning as that, a record
twelve men collected 200-plus hits and Chuck Klein drove in 170 runs
only to finish second in that department—trailing Hack Wilson by a
distant 21 ribbies.

Still, Terry always hit the ball with authority. Pitching great Dizzy
Dean recalled, "He once hit a ball between my legs so hard that my center fielder caught it on the fly backing up against the wall." Dean also
said of Terry, "Could be that he's a nice guy when you get to know him,
but why bother?"

Terry was a vital part of the 1927 Giants. That year, the Yankees
were known as the Murderers' Row due to their powerful lineup, but
the crosstown rival Giants had their own wrecking crew. Anchored by
Terry and Rogers Hornsby on the right side of the infield, the team's

entire inner defense comprised future Hall of Famers, with Travis Jackson at shortstop and Freddie Lindstrom at third. As a unit the four infielders hit a composite .328.

One statement that would haunt Terry came in 1934, when he was the New York Giants player-manager. His team went 93-60, playing superb .608 ball, but only managed to finish in second place. Earlier in the year, when asked about the Dodgers and their chances that season, he replied almost tauntingly, certainly disparagingly, "Is Brooklyn still in the league?" The 1934 Dodgers team *was* poor—they ended the year at 10 games below .500 (71-81), but they were the team that knocked the Giants out of the pennant race.

CHARLIE GRIMM

Philadelphia Athletics 1916; St. Louis Cardinals 1918; Pittsburgh Pirates 1919–1924; Chicago Cubs 1925–1936

The man known as Jolly Cholly was indeed a funny man. Many of his best lines come from his days as a manager, not as a first baseman. Grimm was a baseball "lifer," hitting .290 over twenty seasons and managing an additional nineteen years. He won four pennants with the Chicago Cubs, two as their player-manager, in 1932 and 1935.

He was great with comedic timing. He said of the Waner brothers, Paul ("Big Poison") and Lloyd ("Little Poison"), "Their only weakness is they can't hit balls rolled under the plate."

On another occasion Grimm received a scout's report that stated a minor league pitcher had tossed a perfect game with only one batter hitting a ball, foul at that, out of the infield. Grimm commented, "Forget the pitcher—send the guy who hit the foul."

2

SLUGGERS

Many of the greatest slugging feats in baseball history were accomplished by first basemen. For instance, of the twenty-five men with 500 or more lifetime homers, nine were first-sackers (by our definition) and of the top thirty all-time home run hitters, nearly half, fourteen, were first basemen.

Many years ago Ralph Kiner observed that home run hitters drive Cadillacs, and his observation still holds true. First basemen do command very hefty salaries. In 2010, among all major league regulars, first basemen were the highest-paid players, hauling home on average $9.5 million. Further, nearly a quarter of the highest-paid position players were first-sackers. For the record, Mark Teixeira led the way among men at that position, pulling down $20,625,000 for his 2010 toil. The next highest average belonged to third basemen ($8.47 million) followed by designated hitters ($7.43 million). There was a huge drop-off for the next spot, outfielders ($4.66 million), with shortstops close behind ($4.59 million). At the bottom of the heap were relievers, in 2010 at "only" $2.11 million.

Recent evidence indicates first base has not lost any of its luster as a power spot. In 2010 there were twenty-two men who qualified for the status of full-time first basemen. Of those players, thirteen hit in either the third or the cleanup slot in the lineup. From 2005 through 2010, the NL MVP was a first baseman every season except 2007, when shortstop Jimmy Rollins interrupted the Albert Pujols–Ryan Howard Joey Votto string.

Some of the slugging feats by first basemen were performed over a career, others over the course of a splendid season, and still others were one-shot deals such as Jim Gentile's power explosion of May 9, 1961, when he hit grand slams in the first and second innings in a Baltimore 13–5 rout of the Twins—imagine eight runs driven in after just two innings!

This chapter focuses on many such sluggers and their pyrotechnics.

ERNIE BANKS

Banks ended his glorious nineteen-season career in 1971 with 1,636 runs batted in. The Chicago Cubs legend was inducted into the Hall of Fame as a member of the Class of 1977.

Phil Cavarretta once managed Banks and noted of his unassuming star, "After he hits a homer, he comes back to the bench looking as if he did something wrong." Banks played out that scene 512 times, still twenty-first on the all-time list. Another of his managers, Bob Scheffing, marveled, "You grab hold of him and it's like grabbing hold of steel."

Though then a shortstop, Ernie Banks hit more home runs than any major leaguer from 1955 through 1960, a stellar total of 248, good for an average of just over 41 per season. He would not become a full-time first baseman until 1962, and in fact, he played some left field (23 games in 1961, when fellow future Hall of Famer Billy Williams wasn't patrolling that position), as well as third base for 69 games. He even topped the NL in assists by a first baseman three times in the six seasons he played in 150-plus games at first base.

Play in, say, 2,100 big league games, and there's a very good chance that you make it to at least one World Series somewhere along the line. The list of men with that much regular season experience and none in the Series is rather rare (twenty-seven players through 2009), but for decades Banks headed that group. He played 2,528, all for the Cubs (which helps explains why he was never in the Fall Classic), from 1953 to 1971. A lovable, venerable character, Banks was the recipient of a plethora of pity for holding such a woeful record.

However, that record has been usurped; Banks now stands fourth on the list behind Andre Dawson, at number three; Ken Griffey Jr., at number two; and another first baseman, the most recent leader of this pack, Rafael Palmeiro. From 1986 through 2005 Palmeiro toiled in 2,831 contests, and while he was in the hunt for a World Series ring in 1996 and 1997—both years his Baltimore Orioles lost in the American League Championship Series (ALCS)—and again in 1999 when his new club, the Texas Rangers, lost in the American League Division Series (ALDS), he would never trot out of a dugout and onto a field during a World Series game.

Quite a few other first basemen (defined here as men who played that position in 400 or more contests) are among the top twenty-five in this realm. In fact, 36 percent of these men played first base.

Julio Franco played everywhere on the diamond and the globe. In the majors he played in 2,527 games (making him number five on the no–World Series list) at first base, second, shortstop, designated hitter, and even at third base, left field, and right field.

Only six men are ahead of Rod Carew on this roster of frustration. Carew played in 2,469 big league contests over nineteen seasons, and while he hit a ton, his hopes for Series play were crashed year after year after year.

Meanwhile, Mickey Vernon, number nine on the list, won a batting crown but went 2,409 games without qualifying for postseason play. Frank Thomas (number fourteen at 2,322 games played) and Andres Galarraga at number seventeen (2,257 games) follow Vernon.

Joe Torre, who spent 787 games at first (compared to 903 behind the plate and 515 at third base) was also denied a shot at World Series play and ranks twentieth on that list, although he gained redemption when he led the Yankees to the playoffs seemingly every season he was at their helm (1996–2007). In 1996, his first year as the Yanks skipper, he won the world championship; the Yankees came in second place the next season before running off a tear of three more World Series titles. They then won the pennant two more times over the following three seasons.

For that matter, over Torre's dozen seasons as the Yankees manager, his players won their division every season but two. That's domination.

WILLIE McCOVEY
San Francisco Giants 1959–1973, 1977–1980; San Diego Padres 1974–1976; Oakland Athletics 1976

In his big league debut with the Giants on July 30, 1959, Willie McCovey went 4-for-4 against future Hall of Famer Robin Roberts, including two booming triples. From 1975 through his retirement in 1980 he managed only two triples and averaged almost exactly two triples per season over his twenty-four-year stint. It's noteworthy that even though he didn't get called up to the majors until almost August, he still won the Rookie of the Year Award, unanimously—hitting .354 didn't hurt his cause any.

His power credentials are quite impressive, especially during his years with the Giants—the 1969 MVP led his league in slugging three straight seasons and in homers three times with a high-water mark of 45, helping him accumulate 521 lifetime shots, tied for number eighteen on the all-time list. His 1,555 RBI also helped him become a Hall of Famer. He was so feared he drew a then record 45 intentional walks in 1969 and drew another 40 the next season.

WILL CLARK

In the 1989 NLCS, Clark's bat boomed, almost doing a solo act on the Chicago Cubs. The Giants star, who had lost the batting crown to Tony Gwynn on the final day of the season, went 13-for-20, good for a new League Championship Series (LCS) record .650 batting average over a 5-game set, and established other records with his 24 total bases and his 1.200 slugging percentage. Six of his eight RBI came in one sizzling game, with four of them coming on a grand slam. Not bad for a 1982 graduate of Jesuit High School in New Orleans, the same school attended earlier by fellow slugger Rusty Staub. Incidentally, Clark would go on to become an All-American at Mississippi State University, becoming a teammate with future big leaguers Rafael Palmeiro and Bobby Thigpen.

After Clark came up with his pennant-winning hit, a two-run, bases-loaded single in the eighth inning of the fifth game of the series (he had three of his team's four hits that day), he noted, "If a guy doesn't want to come up in a situation like that, he shouldn't be in the game." Moments prior to his key hit, Clark, who had homered on his first swing as a professional player at Fresno and on his first swing as a big leaguer (against Nolan Ryan), strolled to the batter's box, passing teammate Kevin Mitchell in the on-deck circle. Clark, who had made a jump from Single-A ball to the majors with only 65 minor league games under his belt, was ready to face Cubs closer, the fireballing Mitch Williams. Full of confidence, Clark muttered to Mitchell, "It's done."

His standout play caused San Francisco general manager Al Rosen to gush, "I've seen all the great ones and I've never seen anybody have a series like that." And Clark's manager, Roger Craig, simply said, "You saw the best."

JIM THOME

Cleveland Indians 1991–2002, 2011; Philadelphia Phillies 2003–2005, 2012; Chicago White Sox 2006–2009; Los Angeles Dodgers 2009; Minnesota Twins 2010–2011; Baltimore Orioles 2012

While Jim Thome, who originally broke in at third base with the Cleveland Indians, benefited from manning the designated hitter spot, he had played first in more than 1,100 contests. Through 2012 Thome's home run total stands at 612, ranking him seventh all-time. A feared hitter, he had drawn 1,747 walks, seventh most all-time.

In the first decade of the twenty-first century, the affable Thome, a good friend of legendary basketball coach Bob Knight, starched 368 home runs. Only Alex Rodriguez, with his steroid-tainted 435 blows, hit more. In addition, 12 of Thome's homers were of the walk-off variety, tied for the most ever in the annals of the game. On June 23, 2012,

Thome hit a record-breaking thirteenth walk-off home run. It was also his first pinch-hit home run. He ended the 2012 season with 13 career walk-off home runs.

Some Thome critics pointed to his numerous strikeouts (ranked number two lifetime at 2,548 trailing Reggie Jackson's 2,597), but former minor leaguer Andy Jarvis noted the following:

> I remember listening to an interview with Thome in one of his last years with the Indians. They asked him, "You're leading the league in strikeouts. Do you feel like you should not strike out as much, that you would help the team more if you didn't strike out as much?" And Thome says, "I get paid x amount of millions of dollars. And in my contract the reason why I get paid better [than many other players] is because I hit home runs and drive in runs." And at the time of the interview, he goes, "I'm first in the league in home runs and I'm third in RBI, so I'm doing what I'm getting paid to do." The number, the point 232, or whatever that guy might be hitting, as long as that RBI number [is strong], he's still helping that team.

EDDIE MURRAY

Baltimore Orioles 1977–1988, 1996; Los Angeles Dodgers 1989–1991, 1997; New York Mets 1992–1993; Cleveland Indians 1994–1996; Anaheim Angels 1997

From 1980 through 1989 Eddie Murray had more hits than any man other than Robin Yount. He also ranked third with his 274 home runs, while leading all major leaguers with 996 RBI, good for almost exactly 100 per year over that decade. One time, when the Baltimore Orioles star was in his prime, a survey of ninety-six AL pitchers revealed that these men feared Murray more than any other hitter in the league—he received 21.5 votes to George Brett's 7.5.

On June 30, 1995, Murray became the twentieth player, and just the second switch-hitter ever (joining Pete Rose), to accumulate 3,000 hits. Eight years earlier he had become the first big leaguer to hit homers from both sides of the plate in consecutive contests. To this day only Mickey Mantle hit more switch home runs than Murray.

The taciturn Murray, once described by sportswriter Phil Elderkin as a man "who looks as though he could bend iron bars for a living," also gained fame when he joined two of the game's greatest players ever, Hank Aaron and Willie Mays, as the only men with 3,000 hits and 500 home runs (later Palmeiro would join this group).

Despite all his accomplishments he remains one of the greatest players to have never won an MVP Award. As multitalented as he was, he rarely managed to lead his league in any major offensive category—although he did lead the American League once in on-base percentage, walks, home runs, and RBI. The Hall of Famer Steady Eddie simply plugged away, putting up solid numbers every year. In fact, his best single season hit output was 186, which stood as the lowest total for any player in the 3,000 hit club. Still, look at his 1,917 runs batted in (most ever by a switch-hitter) and his 560 doubles, and toss in his three Gold Gloves, and it's obvious Murray was an all-time great. He even holds the record for the most lifetime assists by a first baseman and once posted a fielding percentage of .999 (during one of three seasons in which he led the AL in fielding), facts few fans realize.

By 1995 Ted Williams stated that while he believed Mickey Mantle was the greatest switch-hitter of all time, Murray and his statistics "are starting to be alarmingly close [to those of the Mick]." Longtime Murray teammate Cal Ripken Jr. recognized that many people never got to know Murray, primarily because he refused to speak with the media, contending that Murray "has the heart of a lion."

LANCE BERKMAN
Houston Astros 1999–2010; New York Yankees 2010; St. Louis Cardinals 2011–2012

A member of the 300 home run club, Lance Berkman gained most of his fame with the Houston Astros. Berkman holds switch-hitting records for the most doubles in a season and the most extra base hits in a year. In 2006 he became one of just a handful of switch-hitters to put up a 40-plus home run season. That was also the year he established an NL record for the most runs driven in (136) by a switch-hitter. During the first decade of the twenty-first century only eight men crushed more homers than Berkman.

DARRELL EVANS
Atlanta Braves 1969–1976, 1989; San Franciso Giants 1976–1983; Detroit Tigers 1984–1988

Darrell Evans played for many clubs in the majors, beginning with the Atlanta Braves. He celebrated his forty-first birthday as a member of the Detroit Tigers by homering and lasted in the game until he was forty-two. Evans swatted 60 homers while in his forties, the third highest total ever. Not only was he the first man to hit 40-plus HR in both leagues, he was also, at thirty-eight, the oldest player to ever win a home run crown.

His favorite batting coach was his mother. Back in the early part of the 1974 season, when he was with his first club, the Atlanta Braves, Evans was mired in a slump. Looking for solace, he called his parents and informed his father of his woes.

His dad listened for a short while, then said, "Hang on just a minute, Darrell. I'll get your mom on the line so she can give you a few tips." It helped, of course, that his mother had once been a member of the Orange County Lionettes, a professional softball team in California.

Her advice helped Evans work his way out of his slump as the month of May rolled around. His batting average had plunged to a nadir of .161 on April 26. By season's end he improved by nearly 80 points.

As a teammate of Hank Aaron's in 1974, Evans was on base the night Aaron smashed the record for the most lifetime homers. A year earlier, Evans, Aaron, and Davey Johnson each hit 40-plus home runs, making them the first trio of teammates to hit that level in a season.

Overall, Evans wound up with 414 homers and 1,354 RBI. Among men with 400 or more home runs who are eligible for Hall of Fame induction, only two—Evans and Dave Kingman—have not received that honor.

JOHNNY MIZE
St. Louis Cardinals 1936–1941; New York Giants 1942–1949; New York Giants 1949–1953

Mize, the original "Big Cat," was the type of slugger whom managers "hid" at first base. Considered a liability with the leather, he once became the butt of a joke when a writer sent a letter to Leo Durocher, Mize's manager with the Giants. It read: "Before each game an announcement is made that anyone interfering with or touching a batted ball will be ejected from the park. Please advise Mr. Mize that this doesn't apply to him."

Still, put a bat in Mize's hand, and it was a vastly different story. The Hall of Famer tattooed 359 lifetime homers while maintaining a .312 career batting average. He made the All-Star team ten times, doing so in virtually every full season he spent in the majors. His 51 home runs in 1947 represented the most ever hit by a National League first baseman. Four times he led or tied for the lead in his league for homers and three times in RBI and total bases. His stats would have been even more impressive had he not lost three prime baseball years while serving in the U.S. Navy.

Although he never got a sniff of postseason play until he was thirty-six years old, once he joined the Yankees in 1949 he won five straight World Series, then retired.

STEVE GARVEY
Los Angeles Dodgers 1969–1982; San Diego Padres 1983–1987

Steve Garvey once noted, "The difference between the old ballplayer and the new ballplayer is the jersey. The old ballplayer cared about the name on the front. The new ballplayer cares about the name on the back."

Garvey certainly was a gamer, breaking the record for the most consecutive games played by a National Leaguer, a mark formerly held by a couple of durable sluggers—first Stan Musial, then Billy Williams. Garvey's string was snapped at 1,207 (still the most ever in NL play) only when he broke his hand.

In the decade of the 1970s, a period in which Garvey played for the Los Angeles Dodgers, he pounded out five seasons with 200 or more hits. In 1974, he not only made the NL All-Star squad, he did so as a write-in candidate. Then, as if to validate his selection to the team, he won that game's MVP Award. From there he went on to become that season's NL MVP.

As a child Garvey grew up around the Dodgers, one of the two teams he would later play for, because his father drove the team's bus in spring training. Steve became a fixture at the Dodgers camp and on road trips. Later he would become part of an infield that played together for nine seasons, an incredible stretch of excellence that featured the team winning four NL flags. That quartet also included Davey Lopes at second, Bill Russell at short, and Ron Cey at third. Garvey wound up his career with 272 homers and 1,308 RBI.

JOEY VOTTO
Cincinnati Reds 2007–2012

Joey Votto, the NL MVP in 2010 as a member of the Cincinnati Reds, is seen as a true up-and-comer. He took home his MVP honors by a margin of 443 votes to 279 for Pujols, emerging as a recognizable force in baseball. Additionally, Votto ranked first, second, or third in his league for on-base percentage, homers, slugging, batting, and runs batted in. With such stats he, like Pujols, became a viable threat to win a Triple Crown.

In 2010, while Pujols finished first in home runs and runs driven in but "only" sixth in hitting, Votto's performance was slightly more balanced, so to speak—he finished second in batting and third for homers and ribbies. Both men's chances for a Triple Crown evaporated as the season wore down, but it was a three-man show (Carlos Gonzalez won the batting title and came in second for RBI and fourth for home runs) while it lasted.

JOE ADCOCK

Cincinnati Reds 1950–1952; Milwaukee Braves 1953–1962; Cleveland Indians 1963; Los Angeles Angels 1964; California Angels 1965–1966

When Joe Adcock was a teammate of Hank Aaron's on the Milwaukee Braves, he got to see close up just how great Aaron was. Some sources say it was Adcock who came up with the classic line, "Trying to sneak a pitch past Hank Aaron is like trying to sneak the sunrise past a rooster."

Adcock was no slouch with the bat. On the final day of July in 1954 he put on a one-man show never to be forgotten. Against the Brooklyn Dodgers in old Ebbets Field Adcock blistered the ball, hitting a double and four, count 'em, four home runs, good for a then record 18 total bases. That mark stood for nearly a half century until Shawn Green went 6-for-6 with a single, double, and four homers on May 23, 2002.

Upon Adcock's retirement only six right-handed hitters owned more home runs than his 336 shots. Further, Adcock was the first of only three major leaguers to hit a baseball so deep it went over the screen and into the very distant (around 500 feet from home plate) center field bleachers of the Polo Grounds (in 1953).

Another big thumper, Cleveland Indians first baseman Luke Easter was actually the first man to reach that area, doing so in 1948 in a Negro League contest. Incidentally, Easter was also the man who came the closest to being the only player to hit a homer into the center field bleachers in Cleveland Municipal Stadium.

Back to the Polo Grounds. The other two men to reach that park's center field bleacher seats were Lou Brock, a seemingly unlikely candidate to do so (he averaged only about 7 homers per season), and Hank Aaron. What was so remarkable about the last two blows is that the park had a long history, and hitting a ball to those bleachers had been proven over and over again to be virtually impossible—and yet Brock, then Aaron connected in back-to-back contests on June 17 and 18, 1962.

JIM BOTTOMLEY

St. Louis Cardinals 1922–1932; Cincinnati Reds 1933–1935; St. Louis Browns 1936–1937

Jim "Sunny Jim" Bottomley, a magnificent player for the St. Louis Cardinals, was hardly a prototypical slugger, hitting just 219 homers over sixteen seasons. Still, he belongs in this chapter because of his 60 homers and 173 RBI over the two-year span of 1928–1929 and for his showing in his greatest game ever. On September 16, 1924, Bottomley became the first man ever to drive home 12 runs in a game (only Mark Whiten has since matched that feat) on a 4 home run performance.

In the decade of the Roaring Twenties Bottomley and Lou Gehrig tied for the most homers by a first baseman (146) despite the fact that Bottomley didn't play full time until 1923 and Gehrig had to wait until 1925 before he became a starter. The winner of the 1928 MVP trophy, the year he led the league in homers with 31, Bottomley went on to amass 465 career doubles and 151 triples, hit .310, and drive in 1,422 runs on his way to becoming a Hall of Famer.

MARK McGWIRE

Oakland Athletics 1986–1997; St. Louis Cardinals 1997–2001

RAFAEL PALMEIRO

Chicago Cubs 1986–1988; Texas Rangers 1989–1993, 1999–2003; Baltimore Orioles 1994–1998, 2004–2005

Collectively, the lifetime homer output of Mark McGwire and Rafael Palmeiro is 1,152 (583 by McGwire). However, their combined percentage of votes for Hall of Fame consideration is paltry—the writers who cast ballots see them as pariahs. In 2010 Big Mac received a mere 23.7 percent of the votes, way short of the 75 percent necessary for induction into the Hall, and he saw that number plunge to 19.8 percent during the following voting period, less than a year after he finally confessed that he had taken steroids and human growth hormones. In

Palmeiro's first year of being eligible for Hall of Fame consideration (2011) he was named on a mere 64 of 581 ballots cast (just 11 percent).

One voter, Susan Slusser of the *San Francisco Chronicle*, indicated she would not vote "for any player connected with steroid use, because I believe cheaters shouldn't be rewarded with the sport's highest honor." She added that such men "can enjoy the big contracts they earned as a result, but they won't get my vote." The election results seemed to send the message that the voters are "reluctant to choose bulky hitters who posted big numbers in the 1990s and 2000s."

Before the truth about McGwire came out, he made a comment that, in retrospect, took a lot of nerve. "Some people are put on this earth to do certain things. He picked Sammy [Sosa] and me to do this [chase and break the season home run record]."

The feats and reputations of McGwire and Palmeiro were stained by their taking performance-enhancing drugs and by their pathetic appearances at a congressional hearing in 2005. Palmeiro emphatically insisted, "I have never used steroids. Period," only to fail a drug test that led to a suspension several months later. McGwire repeatedly informed the House committee that he was "not here to talk about the past." Did he somehow believe the senators brought him to Washington, D.C., to talk about the future?

Despite Palmeiro's status as just one of four men to collect 500-plus HR and 3,000 or more hits, and despite McGwire's record-setting 70 homers in 1998 (when he broke the mark that had been held by Roger Maris for thirty-seven years, as early in the season as September 8) and 65 more the following season, these two first-sackers are little more than symbols of the steroid era.

To many it seems as if McGwire, and later Barry Bonds, had orchestrated Joe Hardy–like deals with the devil, exchanging their baseball souls for an elixir that boosted their home run totals to ungodly heights, permitting them to shatter the records for the most homers in a single season.

In mid-September 2003 Palmeiro joined Jimmie Foxx as the only players ever to post at least 35 HR and 100-plus RBI in nine consecutive seasons. Foxx's muscles and accomplishments, however, were unenhanced.

JEFF BAGWELL
Houston Astros 1991–2005

In January 2011 the results of the voting for the Hall of Fame showed Houston Astros star Jeff Bagwell, in his first year of eligibility, receiving 41.7 percent of the ballots despite putting up stats that the AP called "among the best for first basemen since World War II." He hit just below .300 lifetime at .297 and had a lofty .408 on-base percentage to go with his .540 slugging percentage. He also drove home 1,500 runs and belted 449 homers. While he never tested positive for drugs, the voters were reluctant to endorse him. Bagwell commented, "People are going to have suspicion in the era I played."

Controversy aside, Andre Dawson certainly was impressed by Jeff Bagwell and found him to be an intimidating figure at the plate, capable of launching tape measure shots "because of the type of swing he has. You throw it in his swing and he gets all of it. He's not that big in stature. He's compact, very strong. He's got an uppercut type of swing, and he gets the bat head through the strike zone real quick."

Fellow slugger Joe Carter added, "He's looking for over the roof, over the moon. He hits down in a crouch, but I mean he hits the ball. He's got tremendous hang time."

Bagwell, adept at working the count, possessed a powerful inside-out cut and was an intelligent hitter as well. In all, he collected 449 homers and walked nearly 100 times each season.

JIMMIE FOXX

Foxx was so feared a slugger, on June 16, 1938, the St. Louis Browns almost literally took the bat out of his hands. They may as well have—they walked him six consecutive times, most ever. For the record, Foxx's Red Sox still won the game, 12–8.

In 1940 Foxx hit his 500th homer, extending the membership in the 500 home run club to two. As of 2010, that elite group has swelled to 25, with seven of the sluggers either proven to have been, or suspected of being, aided by performance-enhancing drugs.

From 1929 through 1941 Foxx posted 100-plus RBI each year, an amazing run of thirteen years of superb slugging, good for a record that remained through 2010 (tied with Lou Gehrig, 1926–1938, and later tied by Alex Rodriguez in 2010).

In 1932, the year Foxx slammed 58 home runs for the Philadelphia Athletics, and in 1933, this lifetime .325 hitter who won two batting crowns copped back-to-back MVP titles. What made this unusual— aside from the fact that he was the first man to accomplish this feat— was that he became the first of a dozen players to do this, and that the first nine men on that illustrious list could have fielded a sort of dream team. That is to say, the elite nine played the nine defensive positions of baseball.

Foxx, whose .609 lifetime slugging percentage is the fifth best ever (he topped .700 in slugging a stunning three times), won his awards as a first baseman even though he began his career as a catcher. In fact, despite his value to his teams, he was called upon to don the tools of ignorance, fielding a dangerous position, in 108 games. Foxx even caught in one game as late as 1944 when he was thirty-six years old. He played seven different positions over his twenty-year career, handling chores everywhere except in center field and at second base. He pitched in one game in 1939, and in nine games, including two starts, during his final season six years later, when big league talent was still somewhat diluted owing to a number of players still serving in World War II. Over a total of 22 innings the slugger/hurler posted a 1–0 record with a stellar 1.52 ERA, striking out 10 but walking 14 batters.

In the first of his MVP seasons he spent 13 games at the hot corner, and the following season he even played shortstop in a game, the only time he ever manned that spot. Still, the bulk of his career, 1,919 of his 2,200 games played, was spent at first base.

Subsequent players to win consecutive MVP honors were pitcher Hal Newhouser in 1944 and 1945; catcher Yogi Berra in 1954 and 1955; and outfielder Mickey Mantle in 1956 and 1957, giving the Yankees a stranglehold on MVP honors. Ernie Banks, then a shortstop, earned MVP trophies in 1958 and 1959, and Roger Maris followed suit the following two seasons as an outfielder. Next came second baseman Joe Morgan of Cincinnati's Big Red Machine in 1975 and 1976. Third baseman Mike Schmidt won the award in 1980 and 1981, and Dale Murphy rounded out the outfield and completed the squad of nine men to win two back-to-back MVP Awards in 1982 and 1983. The odds of these nine men not only winning baseball's top honor but also playing the nine spots on the diamond seem astronomical.

Outfielder Barry Bonds accomplished the back-to-back feat in 1992 and 1993, but went even further when he won MVPs from 2001 through 2004.

Another first baseman, Frank Thomas, added his name to the roster in 1993 and 1994. Further, in 1993 Thomas became just the fifth man (and third first baseman) to hit .300-plus with 20 or more homers, 100-plus RBI, 100 or more runs scored, and 100-plus walks drawn over three consecutive seasons, thereby joining Gehrig, Foxx, Ruth, and Ted Williams.

Like Williams, Thomas refused to offer at pitches just one millimeter off the plate. Pitchers realized they either had to serve up hittable pitches or issue walk after walk to the man known as the Big Hurt. Jack Morris, winner of 254 games, summed up pitchers' frustrations with Thomas this way: "It's not fair for a guy to be that strong and yet so disciplined at the plate. I have no idea how to get him out."

Finally, yet another first-sacker joined the group in 2008 and 2009 when Albert Pujols turned the consecutive MVP trick.

ALBERT PUJOLS
St. Louis Cardinals 2001–2011; Los Angeles Angels of Anaheim 2012

By the age of twenty-two St. Louis Cardinals sensation Albert Pujols, a man who remarkably wasn't selected until the 402nd overall pick in the 1999 draft, had already become the first big leaguer to bat .300 with 30 or more homers and 100-plus RBI and runs scored in both of his first two seasons. He had also set an NL record for the most RBI by a rookie (130). From there the NL 2001 Rookie of the Year continued to hit those plateaus with a nonchalance bordering on ho-hum regularity; his ascension to superstar status was simply staggering. Only a 99-run season in 2007 stopped him from extending that fantastic streak from the start of his career through 2011. Furthermore, in 2012, despite getting off to a slow start, he recorded another 100-RBI season, meaning he has been good for 100 or more runs driven in every year he's played except one (he drove in "only" 99 runs in 2011).

He was so spectacular that by 2003, in his third year in the big leagues, Cardinals manager Tony La Russa, who at that point had managed twenty-four years in the majors, called Pujols the best player he had ever managed. For Pujols an off season still produces 30 home runs, 85 runs, and 99 RBI, through 2012 his lowest outputs in those departments.

By the end of 2008 only Hall of Fame slugger Ralph Kiner had compiled more homers (329), than Pujols (who had 319) over the first eight seasons of a career. In 2009, Pujols tied Lou Gehrig's record for the most consecutive seasons (nine), with 30 or more homers and 100-plus RBI while hitting .300 or better. The following season Pujols snapped that tie.

On July 29, 2010, Pujols played in his 1,500th game. At that point in his career he was a .331 lifetime hitter (exactly the same average as fellow St. Louis great Stan Musial and the best average among active players). Pujols also produced 389 homers, 1,183 RBI, and 1,132 runs. Only Ruth, Ted Williams, and two other first basemen, Foxx and Gehrig, were .330 (or better) hitters with 300-plus HR and 1,000 or more runs and ribbies over their first 1,500 contests.

Marvelous accomplishments continued to tumble for the slugger like a tower of children's building blocks. Less than one month later, on August 26, at the age of thirty years and 222 days, he became the third-youngest player to reach the 400 home run level, trailing only Alex Rodriguez and Ken Griffey Jr.

The litany of statistical achievements rolls on. He now holds the record for the most home runs set over a player's first ten seasons in the majors (408), and he is the only player to hit 30 or more homers in each of his first ten years. By way of contrast, Ken Griffey Jr. had 58 fewer homers over his first ten years in the big leagues and Eddie Mathews, second on this list, is a distant 38 home runs behind Pujols.

In addition, Pujols ranks first for the most extra base hits over the period of a player's first ten seasons. He churned out 849 extra base hits, almost exactly 100 more than the number-two man on this list, the legendary Ted Williams (750).

Two of the highest slugging percentages for a player's first ten years belong to first basemen: Lou Gehrig at .640 and Pujols at .624, with Williams sandwiched in between at .633. It's easy to see how over his first ten seasons Pujols won the Silver Slugger as the best offensive player at his position six times. From his rookie season through 2010 he single-handedly produced 16 percent of his team's runs driven in, and an unbelievable 23 percent of all the home runs hit by the Cardinals.

Younger fans think of the prolific Pujols strictly as a first baseman, but he has been versatile enough to play third base and in the outfield. In fact, as a rookie he played at all three of these positions.

Still, first base is where he has hauled home the most honors and records. He is one of just four first basemen to win more than one MVP and the only one from the National League to do so—the others were Foxx, Gehrig, and Frank Thomas.

Starting with his rookie year Pujols has the following finishes in the MVP balloting: fourth, second, second, third, first, second, ninth, first, first, second, fifth, and second in 2011. That's a sensational string of top ten finishes—he was in the top five nearly every one of those seasons. Such a feat illustrates just how integral he is to his team, his place among the baseball's elite, and how he vies for the MVP Award every single season. Through 2010 only Barry Bonds and Stan Musial were more dominating in MVP voting.

Speaking of every single season, through 2010 Pujols had been an All-Star each and every year with the exception of 2002, when he went on to finish second in the MVP voting.

Then there was his unfathomable showing in Game 3 of the 2011 World Series when Pujols led his Cardinals to a 16–7 shellacking of the Texas Rangers. Pujols ripped 5 hits, three of them home runs (joining only Babe Ruth and Reggie Jackson as men to homer three times in a World Series—Pablo Sandoval has since added his name to this elite group), compiled 6 RBI, and established a new World Series record of 14 total bases. It was, quite simply, one of the greatest displays of hitting in postseason history. The Cards went on to win the world championship in seven games.

Trying to find a flaw in Pujols's game is as futile as trying to spin straw into gold. Most sluggers today whiff 100 to 200 times per season.

Pujols has never whiffed more than 93 times—he did so as a rookie—and he averages around 65 strikeouts per season. In short, Pujols inspires fear. Outfielder Ryan Church once observed that even when Pujols hits "a ground ball, it's a freaking missile."

FRANK THOMAS

Chicago White Sox 1990–2005; Oakland Athletics 2006, 2008; Toronto Blue Jays 2007–2008

In 1994 the hulking Frank Thomas of the Chicago White Sox told *Sports Illustrated* he didn't focus on slugging. "I don't especially care about the home run title because people will say, 'Dang. Six-five, 275 pounds. He's supposed to win that.' I'd rather have the hitting title." Thomas, much more than merely a slugger, got his crown in 1997 when he hit .347, four years after he had become the first player since Ted Williams in 1957 to post a slugging percentage above .700—Thomas checked in at a sterling .729.

He also led his league in on-base plus slugging four times. Former manager Jim Fregosi marveled at Thomas's ability to reach base: "This guy has the eye of a leadoff man." In 1994, Thomas nearly reached base in half of his plate appearances, once again something no player had done since Williams. Surprisingly, though, Thomas, who led the AL in walks drawn four times, never did top the league in homers, finishing second twice.

ADAM DUNN

Cincinnati Reds 2001–2008; Arizona Diamondbacks 2008; Washington Nationals 2009–2010; Chicago White Sox 2011–2012

Ask most fans to name all of the players who have cranked out, say, 30 or more home runs each year over their first ten seasons in the majors, and you may find a fan or two who can name three or four of these men. Chances are, though, they will not name outfielder/first base-man/designated hitter Adam Dunn, even though he's right there among all the great sluggers. From his rookie season of 2001 spent with the Reds through 2010, the muscular Dunn, who is 6-foot-6 and 285 pounds, propelled more than 35 homers per season on average. As potent as Ryan Howard, Dunn, just ten days older, had 354 career home runs to Howard's 259 through 2010 (albeit with many more at bats than Howard). By the end of 2012 Dunn escalated his career home run total to 406 after he added 41 shots in 2012, rebounding from a miserable 11 home run season in 2011 (although he did strike out 222 times in 2012, the second highest total for a single season ever).

The 2011 season had been such a fiasco that Dunn, fresh off signing a four-year contract for $56 million in the offseason, wound up hitting .159 to go with his 177 strikeouts. His batting average represented the worst ever for a single season by a man with enough at bats to qualify for the batting title. Furthermore, he became just the second player ever with more strikeouts than points in his batting average (another sometime first baseman, Mark Reynolds, was the first big league player to do this).

Going into 2011 Dunn had strung together seven straight seasons with at least 38 homers—that tied him with Babe Ruth for the second-longest such streak, behind only the nine years Rafael Palmeiro once ran off. That season, however, Dunn couldn't even muster a slugging percentage (.277) higher than his on-base percentage of .292. Against lefties he hit a microscopic .064 on just 6 hits all year long. Entering the 2013 season fans had to wonder which Dunn would show up at the ballpark.

As a high school quarterback, Dunn threw 44 touchdown passes and accounted for almost 4,800 yards through the air. He then attended the University of Texas, where he became friends with teammate Ricky Williams, a running back who would go on to win the 1998 Heisman Trophy. Dunn gave up his football days after one season backing up Major Applewhite and soon moved on to the majors with the Reds.

As is the case with most sluggers, Dunn whiffs quite often. In 2004 his 195 strikeouts broke the record for the most strikeouts in a season previously held by Bobby Bonds. Dunn took his futility mark good-naturedly, saying, "At least that's one Bonds I have a record over."

MARK TEIXEIRA

Texas Rangers 2003–2007; Atlanta Braves 2007–2008; Los Angeles Angels of Anaheim 2008; New York Yankees 2009–2012

In August 2010 Mark Teixeira joined Pujols, Eddie Mathews, and Darryl Strawberry as the only players to scorch 25 or more homers in each of his first eight seasons in the majors, he extended the streak in 2011 (39 HR) before barely falling short of the 25 home run plateau with 24 in 2012, and he tied for the AL lead in homers in 2009. Through 2012 his home run total stood at 338.

Another record the man with eight 100-RBI seasons over his first ten years in the majors holds, which seems underappreciated, is the one for the most ribbies in a season by a switch-hitter, 144 in 2005 with the Texas Rangers. That figure, by way of comparison, is 14 more than Mickey Mantle ever drove home.

Growing up, Teixeira's favorite player was Don Mattingly, who, at one point, wound up as a Yankees coach. Teixeira has worn jersey number 23 as homage to the former Yankees first baseman.

Teixeira played his college ball at Georgia Tech, where he became one of just three Atlantic Coast Conference players to maintain a .400 (or better) lifetime batting average.

DON MATTINGLY

New York Yankees 1982–1995

While hardly a Ruthian slugger with only 222 homers, Yankees star Don Mattingly had some clout in his bat (442 lifetime doubles), and on July 18, 1987, he tied a thirty-one-year-old record when he homered in his eighth consecutive game. That mark was established by Dale Long and later tied by Ken Griffey Jr.

Long noted of his power production (and of his first base position), "You can shake a dozen glove men out of a tree, but the bat separates the men from the boys." By Long's reckoning Mattingly was a man among men. One of baseball's greatest closers, Lee Smith, said that

Mattingly excelled because he "would foul off really good pitches until the pitcher made a mistake or you made a pitch that [he] could hit."

CECIL FIELDER

Toronto Blue Jays 1985–1988; Detroit Tigers 1990–1996; New York Yankees 1996–1997; Anaheim Angels 1998; Cleveland Indians 1988

PRINCE FIELDER

Milwaukee Brewers 2005–2011; Detroit Tigers 2012

In the outfield you've got the Ken Griffey Sr. and Jr. and the Bobby and Barry duo. On the mound you've got Phil and Joe Niekro and Gaylord and Jim Perry. When it comes to two slugging relatives who have both played first base, the Fielder father-son duo stands out.

On the final day of the 1990 season Cecil Fielder of the Detroit Tigers needed a home run to become just the eleventh man to pound 50-plus homers in a year. He turned the trick and tossed in a bonus homer to end up with 51 homers while leading the big leagues in RBI for the first of three straight years, something that only he, Ty Cobb, and Babe Ruth had ever done in AL play.

What made these statistics even more noteworthy is that from 1985 to 1988 Fielder had just 31 home runs over 506 at bats, all with the Toronto Blue Jays. A 1989 stint in Japan, where he began to blossom (38 HR for the Hanshin Tigers), led to his acquisition by Detroit, where he gained his early big league fame.

Cecil hit many a tape measure shot; one of his most famous sailed over the left field roof of Tiger Stadium. Only the burly Fielder and two other men who spent time as first basemen, Harmon Killebrew and Frank "Hondo" Howard, have ever cleared that distant target. Hall of Fame broadcaster Ernie Harwell said of Cecil, "I don't see anybody day in and day out who hits the ball as hard as he does."

In 1991 Fielder hit a ball Rick Dempsey called "the longest ball I ever saw. He hit it out of the entire stadium [Milwaukee County Stadium]. . . . It just disappeared into the night." Dempsey recalled the ball sailing 30 feet above the 8-foot-high fence that stood atop the last row of bleacher seats in left field. "It went halfway up the light tower."

Pyrotechnic displays come naturally to this family. When Prince was young he would accompany his father, known to his peers as Big Daddy, to the ballpark, and occasionally take batting practice. When he was just twelve years old he ripped his first batting practice homer, one that sailed into the upper deck at old Tiger Stadium, quite a shot for any hitter.

Many years later, in 2007, Prince Fielder blasted 50 HR to lead the league. He and his father are the only father-son duo to reach that level.

The two Fielders have the size to go with the job: Cecil was listed as a 240-pounder during his playing days (but later ballooned up to around 280) and Prince checked in at 255 by the time he turned eighteen (down from an ursine 306 pounds when he was a high school sophomore). Surprisingly, Cecil played point guard in high school basketball, and did it quite well—averaging 27 points, 12 rebounds, and 10 assists per game.

Equally surprising facts: (1) in 1988 Cecil once played a game at second base, and (2) his career stolen base total is two. Remarkably, both steals came in 1996 when manager Buddy Bell gave the lumbering Fielder the green light even though Fielder had played 1,097 games without a steal and had been caught stealing in all of his previous four attempts. After his first steal he joked that he had "been working hard on my jumps the last nine years." The second base umpire that day laughingly called Fielder's steal "bigger than Nolan Ryan's seventh no-hitter."

One startling contrast between the slugging father and son is that Cecil was drafted in the thirty-first round in 1981 and wasn't offered a bonus, while Prince, the seventh pick in the June 2002 draft when he was coming off a .524 senior season with 41 RBI in just 82 at bats, accepted a $2.4 million signing bonus, with his father acting as his agent.

Yet another contrast is on display with one glance at the two men's lifetime batting averages: .255 for Dad versus .287 for the son, coming off a personal high of .313 in 2012.

FRANK HOWARD

Los Angeles Dodgers 1958–1964; Washington Senators 1965–1971; Texas Rangers 1972; Detroit Tigers 1972–1973

Frank "Hondo" Howard, who stood 6-foot-7, was a Second-Team All-American at Ohio State in basketball the year he averaged 20.1 points per game and 15.3 rebounds. In the baseball majors, he slashed out 382 homers, including 10 over a 20 at bat spree, with at least one home run coming in each contest during a 6-game span in May 12–18, 1968, giving him the most homers ever for one week.

Teammate Dick Bosman remembered the final shot, one launched out of Tiger Stadium like a cannon burst: "Mickey Lolich tried to sneak a fastball past him. Frank top-handed that ball. It had top spin on it and was kinda' hooking—you hit it hard when it does that. It hit the roof, and BOINK, gone!" Over the long history of Tiger Stadium only four men, all first basemen, ever cleared the left field roof: Howard, Frank Thomas, Cecil Fielder, and Mark McGwire.

Howard spent most of his career with the Dodgers and the Washington Senators. Also known as the Capital Punisher and the Washington Monument, he led his league in homers in 1968 and 1970, with 44 shots each year. In 1969 he hit a personal high of 48, which placed him second after Harmon Killebrew.

HARMON KILLEBREW

Washington Senators 1954–1960; Minnesota Twins 1961–1974; Kansas City Royals 1975

Harmon Killebrew became the first Hall of Famer never to have recorded a season with a batting average of .300 or better—.288 was his best mark. In fact, when he entered Cooperstown, his .256 lifetime average was the lowest of any position player ever inducted into the Hall—but, make no mistake, the man could put a hurt on a baseball.

Interestingly, though, the man who would wind up stealing just 19 bases over twenty-two seasons, spent mostly with the Minnesota

Twins, made his debut as, of all things, a pinch runner, doing so in the first big league game he ever witnessed.

A former high school All-American quarterback, "Killer" amassed 573 home runs, which places him as the eleventh most productive slugger ever. When he retired, only Babe Ruth had more homers in AL play than Killebrew. Six times he led or tied for the lead in his league for the most long balls—the first time he managed this was in his first full season in the majors—and twice he knocked on the 50 home run door, winding up with a personal high of 49 homers. He hit 30 or more homers ten times, and upon his retirement, only Babe Ruth and Ralph Kiner had better ratios for hitting home runs than Killebrew's one home run per each 14.22 at bats. He also left the game with more homers than any other right-handed hitting American Leaguer. In addition, no man hit more home runs than Killebrew in the decade of the 1960s, and he capped off that ten-year span in 1969 by winning the MVP Award, leading the league with a career best 140 RBI.

Hall of Fame pitcher Rollie Fingers said of Killebrew, "It didn't make any difference what I threw—he hit it. And it wasn't just that he hit it, it was where he hit it. If he had accumulated frequent-flyer miles on fly balls off me, he could have gone to Europe and back at least four times."

His defense, however, was nothing to boast of. A teammate of his once quipped, "He hasn't got much range, but what he can get to, he'll drop."

MIGUEL CABRERA
Florida Marlins 2003–2007; Detroit Tigers 2008–2012

In 2011 Victor Martinez of the Detroit Tigers said of teammate Miguel Cabrera, "It's kind of sad hitting behind him because you're going to come up a lot of times with the bases empty. It's really unbelievable. I've seen a lot of good hitters with a lot of good teams, but I've never seen anything like him. That man can hit."

Likewise, in 2011 Cleveland Indians manager Manny Acta said laudatory things about the Tigers star. "I'm not afraid to say I fear him. I'm petrified of the guy. It's no disrespect to the guys who hit behind him. We respect everyone, but we fear Miggy and we're not afraid to say it." Such candor is rare, and it was spoken when Victor Martinez was out of the lineup with an injury, but the message was clear: Cabrera is the main man, the one player a team doesn't want to have beat him. As such, Cabrera earns his share of intentional walks. When the Tigers and Indians met for a 2011 series, the one that prompted Acta's comments, Cleveland issued three intentional walks to Cabrera, two coming in the first inning.

Through 2010, two of the fastest players to reach 1,000 lifetime runs driven in were first basemen Jimmie Foxx and Lou Gehrig. Miguel Cabrera had 879 runs batted in by the end of the 2010 season and was still one full season and about another two weeks shy of reaching his twenty-eighth birthday (April 18, 2012). Gehrig was twenty-eight years and 287 days when he collected his 1,000th RBI, making him the fourth quickest to hit that level, and Foxx, the second quickest, was twenty-seven and 236 days, trailing only Mel Ott (twenty-seven years and 94 days). Clearly Cabrera stood a solid chance of driving in his 1,000th run before he turned twenty-eight, putting him in elite company. While Cabrera seldom falls short when it comes to baseball, he didn't quite join the men previously mentioned. He did, though, collect his 1,000th RBI during the week after he had turned twenty-nine, and by the end of the 2012 season his career total rose to 1,123.

Cabrera was also the second player to accumulate his 300th double before his twenty-eighth birthday—Joe Medwick had 305 two-base hits by the end of the 1938 season when he was twenty-six, and added 48 more the following season before he reached the age of twenty-eight. Cabrera's landmark double came early in the 2011 season.

Before moving to third base in 2012, Cabrera was probably the consensus pick as the second most prolific first baseman in the game today (Pujols got the nod for first). He accomplished so much so quickly he was only twenty-seven as the 2011 season began yet found himself almost exactly halfway to the 500 home run plateau, with 247 HR to his credit (that total has now soared to 321 HR).

Now, with a 2012 Triple Crown to his credit—he became the first player to win that honor since 1967—many feel he is the best hitter in baseball. After all, few people can swat 44 homers, drive in 139 runs, and still hit for average (.330, good for his second straight batting title).

This slugger, who has played first, third, and outfield, has also run together a streak of nine seasons with 100 RBI or better, reaching that level in every one of his full seasons in the majors.

Already a seven-time All-Star, he seems like he can do it all. He's a lifetime .318 hitter with clout, averaging around 40 doubles per season. At one time or another he has led his league in batting average, doubles, homers, runs batted in, on-base percentage, on-base plus slugging, total bases, and intentional walks. Experts concur: this man is a future Hall of Famer.

STAN MUSIAL
St. Louis Cardinals 1941–1944, 1946–1963

St. Louis Cardinals great Stan Musial played 1,016 of his 2,907 games at first base during his glorious career. In the 1940s Musial captured three MVP trophies and his name dominated numerous offensive categories. He led the majors in triples with 108 in that decade, had the fourth-best hit total, and finished second among all big leaguers for runs scored, doubles, batting average (.346), slugging percentage, and on-base percentage. In each of the last five categories, his totals ranked as the best in the entire National League.

One of Musial's biggest highlights came on May 2, 1954, when he drilled 5 home runs during a doubleheader. By an odds-defying coincidence, an eight-year-old Nate Colbert was in the stands that day, and eighteen years later he, too, would crack five homers in a twin bill.

It's difficult, though, to focus on a single accomplishment—upon Musial's retirement he held seventeen big league records as well as twenty-nine NL bests and nine All-Star Game records. Plus, only Musial and three other icons of the game, Ruth, Gehrig, and Ted Williams, finished among the top twenty for homers, ribbies, and batting average. Toss in a top twenty finish for lifetime singles and triples as well, and he is the only player who fits the bill.

A lifetime .331 hitter, with seven batting titles to his credit, Musial clouted 475 homers—some of them with interesting tales. For instance, when the 1955 All-Star Game dragged its way into the twelfth inning,

Musial not only ended it with a homer, he predicted the shot, as recounted by Hank Aaron:

> I remember him standing up [in the dugout] and saying, "They don't pay us to play overtime," and he went up and hit a home run. I know a lot of people say Babe Ruth pointed [to where he planned on depositing a home run during the 1932 World Series], but I know Stan called his.

In all, Musial played in 24 All-Star Games, tied for the most ever. A Musial teammate, Wally Westlake, spoke of a time the Phillies

> were pitching the ball out and away from Stan. He hit a couple of balls about 400-and-some feet out there [center field]. He came in and sat down, and he knew that he wasn't picking his pitches right. I'll never forget his words—he said, "Next time up I'll take care of that." That's all he said.
>
> So his next time at bat they put that ball out over the plate again and he hit a screaming bullet in those left field seats.

Ace reliever Elroy Face said that Musial was so tough, the best way to approach him was to retire the men who came up to the plate before him so that the worst possible damage he could do was to hit a solo home run. "It's like it is with Pujols now—you gotta keep guys off base for him."

However, some may argue that Musial's largest baseball legacy was the way he treated the fans. Even after he owned three MVP Awards he did not have an unlisted phone number and would take calls from anybody.

Brooklyn outfielder George Shuba commented, "Everybody just loves Stan Musial. If you ask any ballplayer what kind of guy Stan Musial was, they'll all say he was a great hitter and a great human being."

No mention of the man who compiled 3,630 hits (with exactly half of them coming in home games and the other half on the road) is complete without touching upon his unique batting stance, usually described as "peek-a-boo" or "corkscrew." One writer said of Musial,

"He doesn't look like a hitter, except when he's hitting." Cubs star Phil Cavarretta chimed in, "He was humped up there like the Hunchback of Notre Dame," declaring the stance "unbelievable."

NATE COLBERT

Houston Astros 1966, 1968; San Diego Padres 1969–1974; Detroit Tigers 1975; Montreal Expos 1975–1976; Oakland Athletics 1976

On August 1, 1972, St. Louis native Nate Colbert tattooed 5 home runs and drove in 13 runs in a doubleheader, tying Musial's record for the most homers in a twin bill and shattering The Man's record for ribbies in a doubleheader.

During the 1972 season Colbert drove in 22.7 percent of his Padres runs, still a record according to Colbert's profile on The Baseball Page website. His season highs for homers came in 1970 and 1972 (38 HR), but owning to the length of his career, only 1,004 games over ten seasons, he totaled just 173 homers—with 3 percent of those blasts coming in one day. For that matter, 13 percent of his home runs hit in 1972 came in that splendid doubleheader.

WILLIE STARGELL

Hall of Fame pitcher Don Sutton said of Pittsburgh Pirates standout Willie Stargell, "I never saw anything like it. He doesn't just hit pitchers. He takes away their dignity." He often did so with towering homers. Bert Blyleven recalled one such mammoth blow: "He hit a shot off Wayne Twitchell like a golf shot." It silenced the crowd, said Blyleven, for about fifteen seconds. Andre Dawson called Stargell one of the top three most impressive sluggers he had ever seen.

Stargell is the only man to hit a ball out of Dodger Stadium, and he did so twice. He hit 4 of the 12 home runs that soared into the distant upper deck at Three Rivers Stadium in Pittsburgh, and he hit 7 of the 18 baseballs that cleared the 86-foot-tall right field roof that loomed over the playing field of the Pirates home park of sixty-one years, Forbes Field.

Ron Fairly told *USA Today* that when he played for the Expos, there were occasions "when the Pirates had a two—or three—touchdown lead on us, [and] I would try to talk our catcher John Boccabella into calling for a low fastball to Stargell and to tell him it was coming. I would say, 'John, let's just see how far he could hit it.'"

Stargell hit 475 career home runs, tied with Musial (number twenty-eight all-time). His hitting was so impressive in the 1979 post-season he won the MVP of the NLCS (hitting .455) and the World Series (.400 with three homers), and he tied fellow first baseman Keith Hernandez for regular season MVP honors as well—that year's voting remains the only tie for the MVP. Stargell even topped all hitters for the most homers in the 1970s, with 296.

Ironically, Stargell died the day the Pirates opened their new ballpark, beautiful PNC Park. Now a 12-foot bronze statue of the beloved Pops stands outside that facility.

CARL YASTRZEMSKI
Boston Red Sox 1961–1983

Expectations were always high for Carl Yastrzemski. He was projected to become a star in both basketball and baseball at Notre Dame, but he did so well on the diamond he signed a contract with the Boston Red Sox after his freshman year. The Red Sox organization then expected him to replace Boston legend Ted Williams in left field, and he did so in 1961.

Yastrzemski went on to become a Hall of Famer, winning two batting titles, an MVP trophy, and a Triple Crown along the way. He also became the first American Leaguer with 400-plus homers and 3,000 or more hits, and he won seven Gold Gloves, all for his outfield play.

It's been more than forty years since Yastrzemski won baseball's Triple Crown. What followed are innumerable accounts of a once-in-a-generation/era/lifetime/century 1967 season for the Boston Red Sox. The milestone's been dissected, analyzed, and opined by media and fans alike, time and again. Others have flirted with the Triple Crown feat but had never accomplished it until 2012. The task is so staggering it has come to define a man who played for twenty-three big league seasons.

Upon retiring in 1983, Yastrzemski had this to say:

I think the best way to sum it up is that I wasn't the greatest
home run hitter that ever lived. But I hit home runs. I have the
extra base hits. I have the total bases. I have the RBI. I wasn't
the greatest average hitter that ever lived, but I wasn't too bad.
Three thousand, four hundred base hits. I had walks starting
innings, and they help win ballgames. Defensively, I wasn't bad.

I'd go against anybody in a seven-game series. You put eight
Yastrzemskis out there, I'll take my chances.

What more can be said about the 5-foot-11, 175-pound (give or
take an inch and 5 pounds) Hall of Fame left fielder, who played 27
percent of his games at first base?

Maybe the place to start is saying baseball could use another Yaz—
as he's fondly become known—in the sense that he played his entire
career with one team; his longevity spanned three decades; he had to
work for everything he got.

"Yastrzemski, who played in more American League games than anybody in history, shows us how far dogged willpower can carry a man of
less than superhuman gifts," wrote Thomas Boswell for the *Washington
Post* following Yastrzemski's induction into the Hall of Fame in 1989.

Boswell went so far as to call Yastrzemski a Sisyphus, referring to a
king in Greek and Roman mythology who was charged with rolling an
enormous boulder up a hill, then watch it roll down, only to repeat the
task for eternity, representing Yastrzemski's willingness to continue
laboring in the face of difficult circumstances.

One of baseball's most prominent examples of a player telling his
team, "Jump on my back, boys, and I'll carry us to the World Series,"
came in 1967 when Carl Yastrzemski (almost) did a solo act, lifting his
Boston Red Sox out of a quagmire of teams grappling for the American
League pennant down the stretch run of a wild season.

According to Boswell,

if one moment epitomizes Yastrzemski, it was a hot pennant race
night in Yankee Stadium in 1978. The great left fielder's right

hand bothered him so badly he had a trainer tape the bat into his palm so he could take batting practice without dropping the implement in pain. He reported to the manager's office, demonstrated his invention, and pronounced himself ready to play. "What are you going to do if you hit a double?" manager Don Zimmer said. "Slide into second base with the bat?"

Sure, there were the .326 batting average, 44 home runs, and 121 RBI of 1967, and everything that followed: the remarkable pennant run, Major League's Most Valuable Player Award, and *Sports Illustrated* Sportsman of the Year honor. But 1967 was only Yaz's seventh season in the big leagues—clunkers like 1971 (.254 batting average, 15 home runs, 70 RBI) and 1972 (.264, 12, 68) followed.

After 1970, Yaz hit more than 20 home runs only three times (in thirteen seasons). And outside of his Triple Crown campaign, he never led the league in homers or RBI. But despite inconsistencies, ups, and downs, Yaz kept on grinding, and over time, a lot of time, his numbers stacked up against some of the best: 3,419 hits, 452 home runs, 1,844 RBI.

He received much credit for not only pushing through some tough seasons but also for having to begin his run by replacing the legendary Ted Williams.

Trivia note: in 1968, a year that, due to the domination of pitching over hitting, came to be known as the Year of the Pitcher, Yaz won the batting title, but with the lowest mark ever for a batting champ, .301.

LOU GEHRIG
New York Yankees 1923–1939

Back in the 1950s there was a pitcher named Lew Burdette who had the nickname "Nitro Lew" because he hailed from the town of Nitro, West Virginia. Because of his explosive bat, Yankees legend Lou Gehrig should have been the original "Nitro Lou."

His records are legion. One of the more obscure ones—although it deserves more acclaim—is his 447 total bases in 1927, the most ever for a first baseman and still the third highest ever. That statistic included

60 total bases on his 20 triples, also a high-water mark for AL first base-men. For the record, the 400 total base level has been attained twenty-nine times; Gehrig did this rare feat five times.

Gehrig's first display of big league slugging came on September 27, 1923, when he homered off Boston's Bill Piercy. In an amazing coincidence, his final home run came on the same date fifteen years later off Dutch Leonard, ending his illustrious career with 493 roundtrippers. In between he enjoyed the first modern-day 4 home run game, set a record with his astonishing five seasons with 400 or more total bases, won a Triple Crown, hit .340 lifetime, and racked up 1,995 RBI (number five all-time).

In other words, he is universally recognized as the greatest first base-man ever, even today, decades after he last laced up his spikes. Had he stayed healthy, who knows how much more he would have added to his numbers—his career ended when he was just thirty-five years old.

In 1926, his first full season, he scored and drove in 100-plus runs, beginning a streak that lasted until he fell ill in his final season, 1939. The following season, the year his team was nicknamed Murderers' Row, he won the MVP Award while earning just $8,000 (as contrasted to Ruth's jaw-dropping salary of $70,000). Financial matters could have been, and actually had been, worse for Gehrig—in 1925 he earned $3,750; that figure jumped up to only $6,500 the next year; his highest salary was a mere $39,000; and he only made $360,000 for his entire career—mere chump change nowadays.

The decade of the 1930s belonged to "Larrupin' Lou." His 1,257 runs scored was the best total for that ten-year span and was, in fact, the second-highest number of runs for a decade ever, behind only Babe Ruth and the 1,365 runs he tallied in the Roaring Twenties. Gehrig also had the highest on-base percentage of the 1930s, the second-best slugging percentage and batting average (.343, trailing only fellow first base-man Bill Terry, who hit a gaudy .352), the second-highest home run output (347, behind another first baseman, Jimmie Foxx, who hit 415) and RBI total (1,358—also behind Foxx, who drove in 1,403 runs), the fourth-most hits, and even the eighth-most triples.

In 1930 Gehrig had 117 runs driven in on the road, a total good enough to lead the league for some years. In all he had 174 RBI that season (sixth-best all-time) and improved on that total the following season when he chased home 184 runs, still the second most ever for a single season. He also holds down the number four position on the list for the most RBI in a season (tied with Foxx at 175) as well as the following slots: thirteenth, twenty-second, thirty-seventh, and fortieth—that's seven of the top forty most prolific RBI seasons ever. By way of comparison, Babe Ruth is in the top forty 5 times. As a matter of fact, Gehrig also holds the records for the most seasons with 150-plus RBI (seven) and the most consecutive seasons with 150 or more ribbies (three).

Additionally, his twenty-three grand slams represent a record that has withstood decades of challenges until Alex Rodriguez tied his record. In addition, other threats to share or break Gehrig's record came from Manny Ramirez and two first basemen, Eddie Murray and Willie McCovey. A duo of other first basemen, Travis Hafner and Don Mattingly, hold the record for the most slams in a single season (six), and two other first-sackers, Ernie Banks and Albert Pujols, hold the NL high (five).

Seldom does a player command big, bold headlines by not playing in a given game, but on May 2, 1939, Gehrig's absence from the lineup for the first time in 2,130 games was huge news. His Yankees were playing the Tigers when Gehrig's iron horse trek chugged to a halt. He informed his manager, Joe McCarthy, "I'm out of the lineup. I'm just not doing the team any good." It was only later that pitcher Lefty Gomez could lend some levity to the situation, saying to Gehrig, "It took fifteen years [actually almost fourteen] to get you out of a game. Sometimes I'm out in fifteen minutes."

Gehrig's string of games played actually began on Memorial Day of 1925 when he appeared as a pinch hitter for Pee-Wee Wanninger, the same man who had earlier taken over the shortstop position from Everett Scott. In an odd chain of events, Scott was the player who had held the record for the most consecutive games played (1,307), a record Gehrig would absolutely shatter.

The day after hitting for Wanninger, Gehrig took over the first base job by replacing Wally Pipp, who, suffering from a headache he sustained after being hit in the head during batting practice, had asked his manager for a day off. "I took two of the most expensive aspirins in history," lamented Pipp.

In addition to his feats on the baseball diamond, Gehrig will forever be remembered for his "Luckiest Man" speech, given the day he said farewell to the game he loved so dearly. Nobody could believe that the man writer Jim Murray would later call "a symbol of indestructibility—a Gibraltar in cleats" was dying.

Aside from his streak of consecutive games played, Gehrig's most terrific feat may well be his record-setting lifetime pace of driving in nearly one run per game played over his long career (.92 to be precise).

TONY PEREZ
Cincinnati Reds 1964–1976, 1984–1986; Montreal Expos 1977–1979; Boston Red Sox 1980–1982; Philadelphia Phillies 1983

The steady Tony Perez was a vital, yet somewhat unappreciated, gear in Cincinnati's Big Red Machine. Throughout the 1970s only two men banged out more doubles than Perez's 303, and every season he was good for 90–100 runs driven in—his 954 ribbies for the decade trailed only that of teammate Johnny Bench's 1,103.

A great clutch hitter, Perez ended 11 games over his career with the electrifying suddenness of a home run, good for the seventh-most walk-off homers ever. The Hall of Famer enjoyed seven 100 RBI seasons and finished with 1,652 RBI, through 2012 still the twenty-eighth-highest total ever.

RYAN HOWARD
Philadelphia Phillies 2004–2012

The Philadelphia Phillies massive Ryan Howard won the 2005 Rookie of the Year Award, then upped the ante, winning the 2006 MVP Award. He showed his power potential early and often. On July 16, 2009, he became the fastest player ever in the majors to reach the 200 lifetime home run plateau, breaking the record of Ralph Kiner who, as difficult as it may be to fathom, had captured (or tied for) the home run title in each of his first seven seasons in the majors.

Howard pelted 45 or more homers each year from 2006 through 2009 with a peak of 58 in 2006, and in three of his first four full seasons he drove home 140-plus runs and led the NL in that category. For those who love obscure stats: from 2006 through 2010 no big leaguer hit more than Howard's 84 homers with his team trailing games. Aside from his 108 and 116 RBI seasons in 2010 and 2011 his lowest runs driven in total for a full season was 136.

From 2006 to 2010 Howard had 680 RBI, the most in baseball, and a terrific total of 71 more runs driven in than Pujols, the number-two man on that list. Howard's career home run total through 2012 was exactly 300.

Former minor leaguer Andy Jarvis had observed a young Howard during a spring training game and critiqued the Phillies star:

> He's so big and strong and [with him] it's just effortless. It's God-given with a bunch of power in that body. And he's a good, classic short swing—usually big guys have big, powerful swings, but his is just nice and short and smooth; it doesn't even look like he's trying, and the ball just explodes off his bat.

HANK GREENBERG
Detroit Tigers 1930, 1933–1941, 1945–1946; Pittsburgh Pirates 1947

Detroit Tigers star Hank Greenberg, known as Hammerin' Hank years before Hank Aaron, was promising enough to get a call up for a very quick sip of coffee (one at bat) in the majors back in 1930 at the raw age of nineteen.

By 1935 he was polished; he drove in 170 runs, led his Tigers to their first world championship, and won the MVP unanimously. However, the most incredible thing about that season was that Greenberg came up with 103 RBI in his first 76 games. Only he and Juan Gonzalez (101 RBI over 87 contests in 1998) ever topped the century mark for RBI by the All-Star break. The kicker? He was not on the 1935 All-Star squad.

Greenberg's personal high of 183 RBI in 1937 was the second of three times he would drive in 150 or more runs, and those 183 ribbies still rank third in baseball history for runs batted in during a season.

Three first basemen were on the 1937 All-Star roster for the American League. Lou Gehrig started and Jimmie Foxx came in as a pinch hitter. As for Greenberg—he did not even appear in the game; the RBI factory sat in the dugout all day long. Further, the AL team, under Yankee manager Joe McCarthy, used only one offensive bench player during the entire game, Foxx, and McCarthy dipped into his bullpen twice, but that was it—only twelve men saw action that day for the AL. Nowadays, fans expect to see virtually every All-Star perform, and some players feel snubbed if they don't get at least one token at bat. Managers of All-Star Games delicately balance their duties, mindful of winning the game, but also of appeasing fans and players alike.

Back in 1938 Greenberg had a solid chance to eclipse Babe Ruth's single season home run record, but came up 2 home runs shy at 58. That total is, aside from Mark McGwire's 70 and 65 tainted outbursts, the most ever by a first baseman—Jimmie Foxx also hit 58 in 1932 but 13 of his games that year were spent at third base, and Ryan Howard hit exactly 58 in 2006. At the time Greenberg's 58 homers were also the most ever, tied with Foxx, by a right-handed hitter.

Had Greenberg not missed considerable playing time, mainly due to serving his country in World War II, the powerful right-handed hitter may well have finished his career as a member of the ritzy 500 home run circle. Consider these facts: In 1941 he played just 19 games at the age of thirty. The next time he hoisted a bat in the majors was after the war, in 1945, when he got into just 78 contests, but one of those games, the pennant-clinching one, belonged to Greenberg. He came to the plate in the ninth with his Tigers down by a run and hit a dramatic grand slam to put the AL pennant on ice.

His first full season after the war, 1946, he turned thirty-five years of age on New Year's Day. That year, he jacked 44 home runs, but perhaps because he hit just .277, the Tigers sold him.

Greenberg added 25 homers the following season as a member of the Pirates, then left the game for good. Not many men are through after a 25 home run season with more than 70 runs and ribbies, but Greenberg, a two-time MVP, a future Hall of Famer, and the possessor of 331 lifetime homers, 1,276 RBI, and a career batting average of .313, was through. In fact, his 1947 home run total stood as the most by a player in his final season until Ted Williams hit 29 in 1960, the year he bowed out. When Greenberg retired he had played only seven seasons in which he had 500 or more at bats—in four of those years he led his league in homers and ribbies.

Many fans today may be unaware of his greatness, but his stats, such as his 63 doubles in his first full season, his average of almost one RBI per game played (.915), his number-eight ranking among career leaders for slugging percentage (.605), and his on-base plus slugging (1.017) attest to his batting prowess.

FRED McGRIFF

Toronto Blue Jays 1986–1990; San Diego Padres 1991–1993; Atlanta Braves 1993–1997; Tampa Bay Devil Rays 1998–2001, 2004; Chicago Cubs 2001–2002; Los Angeles Dodgers 2003

For someone who nearly reached the once tried-and-true Hall of Fame benchmark of 500 home runs, it's a wonder why Fred McGriff played for a whopping seven big league clubs during his nineteen-year career. The man who attained national appeal as the "Crime Dog" never spent more than five seasons with the same team despite regularly producing Most Valuable Player–like numbers in both leagues.

A slender slugger, the six-foot-three, 200-pound McGriff became a left-handed commodity en route to 493 career home runs and never suffered the ire that many of the other big boppers of his era did. As contemporaries like Mark McGwire and Barry Bonds swelled statistically, and physically, in McGriff's case only his numbers burst bubbles.

"His statistics rarely fluctuated, and neither did his body," David Whitley wrote for the *Orlando Sentinel* in 2005. "McGriff is the same lanky guy today that he was in 1986."

The mark of consistency, McGriff also flashed versatility. He led both leagues in home runs, ripping 36 for Toronto in 1989 and 35 for San Diego against a new batch of pitchers in 1992, respectable pre–steroid era numbers. McGriff finished sixth in MVP voting both of those seasons and finished in the top ten each year from 1989 to 1994.

Joe Carter, who witnessed McGriff firsthand in 2002 as the Chicago Cubs color commentator on WGN-TV, said that McGriff is the type of hitter who could

> hit the ball out of all parts of the field and sit at home plate and watch it [confident that he's cleared the fence]. He's got that big, huge backswing where he swings and gets a lift [on the ball]. . . . He's probably one of the strongest guys in baseball as far as hitting the ball out of the ballpark.

McGriff's last powerful mark on the game happened to be that 2002 season with the Cubs, and most appropriately, too, as he made more money that season ($7.25 million) than any other, following the trade from Tampa Bay for Manny Aybar and Jason Smith. McGriff hit 30 home runs for the Cubs and eclipsed 100 RBI, by 3 ticks, for the sixth and final time during his nearly two-decade span. He left the Cubs after that season, offering short one-year campaigns (only 369 total at bats) to the Los Angeles Dodgers and the Tampa Bay Rays before retiring at age forty in 2004.

"He amazes me because he doesn't even seem to swing very hard and the ball jumps off his bat," said Andre Dawson, another former Cub who joined the team late in his long career, much like McGriff, and then went on to win the 1987 MVP Award. "Most of his home runs are tape measure."

Clearly a slugger—fellow big batsman Mickey Tettleton quipped that McGriff "hits 'em where most guys need a driver or a three wood to get to"—perhaps the only remaining debate around McGriff is which hat he would don upon entering the Hall of Fame. Of course, his vote percentage will need a boost first. He received only 21.5 percent in 2010 and 17.9 in 2011, partially a result of twice leading the majors in errors among first basemen and eleven times finishing in the top five. But McGriff told the *Philadelphia Inquirer* in 2004 that respect for his numbers may increase because of the attention heavy steroid users have shed on the game.

"Now people might have more respect for me hanging in there instead of asking, 'Fred's not hitting 60. Why?' You can't prove anything, but if it all comes out in the wash, there might be more appreciation for what I've done," McGriff said, adding, "I know how hard it is to hit home runs."

As reporter Jim Salisbury pointed out in that same *Philadelphia Inquirer* article, McGriff's 36 dingers trumped McGwire by 3 for the AL home run title in 1989 and McGriff's 35 HR bettered Bonds by one for the NL title in 1992. However, McGwire hit 70 home runs nine years after his race with McGriff, and similarly, Bonds hit 73 nine years after his battle with McGriff. The Crime Dog stayed clean, while both McGwire and Bonds have been linked to the use of performance-enhancing drugs.

"In 1995, I was asked to do a children's book on the top ten home run hitters of all time," said historian Bill Deane, a former senior research associate at the Hall of Fame, to *Chicago Sun-Times* columnist Greg Couch in 2002:

> They asked me to pick two current players. One of the guys I picked was Fred McGriff.
>
> He had hit 30 home runs seven years in a row back when people weren't doing that. He was on the fast track to the Hall. But then everyone else started hitting homers, and he stopped.

To Deane's credit and, really, McGriff's as well, the selection remains justified, as many of the players who surpassed McGriff have been linked to steroid use.

As for which team McGriff will be associated with most, consider him breaking into the majors and rising to elite status in five seasons with the Blue Jays. At the same time, McGriff played equally as long in Atlanta (1993–1997), absolutely legitimizing his ninth-round draft selection (by the New York Yankees in 1981) as a perennial postseason power hitter—but as more of a Brave for life, so to speak, than a Blue Jay.

In 50 career postseason games over five seasons (four with the Braves), McGriff hit .303 with 10 home runs (22 total extra-base hits) and 37 RBI, numbers that project to more than 30 home runs and 100

RBI over the course of a 162-game regular season. In 12 games over two World Series appearances with the Braves, McGriff hit .279 (only 5 points below his career regular-season average) with 4 home runs, 9 RBI, and 9 runs scored.

In the 1995 series against Cleveland, he posted a .609 slugging percentage (100 points better than his career regular-season percentage) and nearly matched that against the New York Yankees in 1996 with a 600 series mark.

Perhaps it's no wonder, then, why an in-demand McGriff flip-flopped leagues four times and was traded four times. He simply kept producing.

As a trivia sidenote, McGriff is the cousin of two former big league players, Terry McGriff and standout defensive catcher Charles Johnson.

LEE MAY

Cincinnati Reds 1965–1971; Houston Astros 1972–1974; Baltimore Orioles 1975–1980; Kansas City Royals 1981–1982

There's no doubt Lee May was underappreciated by owners, general managers, and fans alike during his time with the Cincinnati Reds. Past teammates found a way to give him a hard time, too, even if it was in good fun.

During shortstop Dave Concepcion's number 13 jersey retirement ceremony in 2007, Concepcion told May, "The only reason you got traded from the Reds was that you couldn't handle my throws." Said May, as reported in the *Dayton Daily News*, "On which bounce?"

May seemed to stand up for himself well enough, but when it comes to trades, players don't have much say. So when Reds general manager Bob Howsam packaged May and others for Houston Astros second baseman Joe Morgan, center fielder Cesar Geronimo, pitcher Jack Billingham, infielder Denis Menke, and outfielder Ed Armbrister in November 1971, May's time with the Big Red Machine was over.

Too bad for May, as the fun in Cincinnati was just about to begin. Under Howsam from 1967 to 1978, the Reds won six division titles, four NL pennants, and two World Series.

An underwhelming opinion of May continued to some degree when he returned to the Reds as a first base coach. Then-owner Marge Schott, as outspoken and controversial as they come in the big leagues, disparaged May and his fellow coaches when she said none of them was fit to replace manager Pete Rose.

When Schott eventually released Lee from his duties, he felt she broke a promise to him. "If baseball is coming to the way this lady is doing things," Lee told the Associated Press, "I don't want any part of it."

The hits kept on coming. When May finally entered the Reds Hall of Fame, it was by way of the veterans committee of the Cincinnati chapter of the Baseball Writers Association of America—not the fans.

"I'm ecstatic. I'd given up; I thought this would never happen," May told the *Dayton Daily News*. "Even though I played the last eleven years of my career with other teams, I'm a lifer with the Reds. I came up with them and played seven years for them. They're my team."

May hit .274 for the Reds from 1965 through 1971 with 147 homers and 449 RBI. Lifetime, he hit .267 with 354 homers and 1,244 RBI. He hit 32 or more homers three straight seasons for the Reds and later recorded hit number 2,000 with Kansas City.

Lee will be remembered, all right. Reds Classic Rewind televised 6 classic Reds games on FOX Sports Ohio. Along with memories like Rose breaking Ty Cobb's hit record and Tom Seaver's only no-hitter, May's clutch-hitting was promoted as the highlight of the Reds 6–5 win over Baltimore in Game 4 of the 1970 World Series, which they lost.

In some good company, May held another "who knew?" slugging record of sorts. Four pairs of teammates have hit back-to-back homers five times: New York Yankees Joe DiMaggio and Lou Gehrig (1938), Cincinnati Reds Johnny Bench and May (1970), Atlanta Braves Bret Boone and Chipper Jones (1999), and Colorado Rockies Larry Walker and Todd Helton (2001). The record has since been broken.

As a trivia aside, he and his brother Carlos set an obscure record in 1970 when they combined for 221 strikeouts by a sibling combo. The record was extended to a staggering 316 by B. J. and Justin Upton in 2010, and that duo now holds down the top three highest combined season strikeout totals by brothers.

CARLOS DELGADO

Toronto Blue Jays 1993–2004; Florida Marlins 2005; New York Mets 2006–2009

The likes of Jeff Bagwell and his extremely uncomfortable-looking batting stance aside, major leaguers make performing their trade look easy, especially left-handed hitters.

Over the years, experts and fans alike have remarked about the smooth-swinging nature of the rare breed that steps into the "other" batter's box. And when they do it with power, as Carlos Delgado did for the better part of two decades, it's something to behold.

Perhaps none said it better than Frank Ahrens in the *Washington Post* more than a decade ago, following an observation of Ted Williams and the other members of "the team of the century" before the start of Game 2 of the World Series at Turner Field:

> There, in black-and-white film, was the Williams swing: a hitchless loop with a slight uppercut, ending with a graceful twist of his spidery frame, uniform number 9 turned to face the umpire.
>
> Now, think of other swings, ones so perfect or majestic or effortless as to stay locked in memory forever, powerful arcs of eternity. The older ones are as fuzzy as daguerreotypes, but consider the swings of: Mel Ott. Lou Gehrig. Stan Musial. Roger Maris. Reggie Jackson. Tony Oliva. George Brett. Tony Gwynn. Darryl Strawberry. Barry Bonds. David Justice. Griffey Jr. Each one of them, like Williams, a lefty.

In the same article, sweet-swinging lefty Will Clark offered simplicity, sounding as dumbfounded as any novice fan would when he said, "For some reason a lefty's swing evolves in a more pleasing-to-look-at fashion."

Despite the beauty, the grace, and the ease with which lefties often perform the near-impossible—the great Williams himself said the hardest thing to do in all of sports is to squarely connect a round bat to a round ball—they know when their skills have subsided and their time is up.

Even Delgado, whose big swing got him signed as a sixteen-year-old undrafted free agent out of Puerto Rico, according to Bruce Feldman of the *Chicago Sun-Times*, can't outrun Father Time.

"There comes a moment when you have to have the dignity and the sense to recognize that something is not functioning," said Delgado, who traded his comeback attempt for retirement in 2011 after logging seventeen years of big league service. "You can't swim against the current."

Beset by injuries, including three hip surgeries in an eighteen-month span in 2009 and 2010, the two-time All-Star ended his career ranked thirtieth of all time for career home runs (473). He never led the league in homers—his career high 44 came in the middle of his twelve years with Toronto—but he did manage three Silver Slugger Awards (1999, 2000, 2003) while playing for the Blue Jays.

As a catcher in the Blue Jays' organization, Delgado may have been more likely to have a squatty batting stance like that of Bagwell. Instead, the converted first baseman made the leap to the big leagues in 1993 with a more upright and natural approach at the plate. Delgado only played in 2 games with the eventual World Series champions that season before becoming a regular in the lineup in 1996, and in Most Valuable Player voting.

Delgado's best season unfolded in 2000 when he collected the Hank Aaron Award for being the best overall offensive performer in the American League.

His .344 batting average, 41 roundtrippers, 137 RBI, and big league best 57 doubles turned out to be a precursor to his most appreciated season—2003. Voted second in the MVP race—behind Alex Rodriguez, who later admitted to using performance-enhancing drugs—Delgado trumped his fourth-place ranking from three years earlier.

While nobody may ever know for certain, Delgado seemed to have taken a more traditional approach compared to Alex Rodriguez when it came to keeping pace with his peers. When his body could no longer keep up, he retired; when expected to carry his team (as New York Mets manager Willie Randolph once stated he hoped he would) but immersed in a slump, Delgado sought that special feeling from within instead of from somewhere else.

"You find that groove, that power swing. It's been that way my whole career," Delgado told the Associated Press, pedaling an exercise bike after breaking out of a rut with a 2 homer game against Florida in 2007. It's also been reported elsewhere that while with Toronto, Delgado rode his mountain bike to the ballpark on game days. "I've been feeling better at the plate. Once you start hitting better, you can find that groove."

Delgado's career numbers were hardly a result of slow and steady annual production, yet he only cracked two All-Star rosters. Even after he left the club that had signed him as an amateur free agent in 1988, Delgado still put up good numbers. In one year with the Marlins (2005) and in the three full seasons with the Mets (2006–2009), he averaged 33 home runs and 108 RBI. And in that last full season, he finished ninth in the MVP race.

But competition was fierce at first base from 1996 through 2004, when Jim Thome twice occupied the starting first baseman's spot in the All-Star Game, and Jason Giambi had it three times. And during Delgado's four full NL seasons (2005–2008) a round-robin of sorts took place at the bag as Carlos Lee, Albert Pujols, Prince Fielder, and Lance Berkman slid in and out of the starter's role around Delgado—who by season's end in three of those years finished in the top twelve for MVP voting.

Any bid for Cooperstown that Delgado may have had may have looked better with more postseason appearances. After his one outstanding season with the Marlins—during which Delgado hit .301 with 33 homers and 115 RBI after taking almost a $16 million pay cut—the "Fish" traded him to the Mets, and Delgado helped them come within a game of the World Series. During 10 postseason games in 2006, Delgado hit .351 (71 points higher than his career average) with 4 home runs, 11 RBI, and posted a slugging percentage of .757 (more than 200 points higher than his career average).

Hal Bodley, *USA Today* baseball writer, MLB.com commentator, and credentialed Hall of Fame voter via membership in the Baseball Writers Association of America, had this to say about Delgado's predicament:

> I think it's really sad he had to end his career the way he did because when he was with Toronto and he was hitting home runs and driving in runs, I thought he was a certain Hall of

Famer, one of the greatest hitters that I'd ever seen at that time. And it's a shame that the injuries and some of the years that he had with the New York Mets are gonna tank that career a little bit. But he was really a great hitter.

Through 2010, Delgado remains the last player to hit four home runs in one game. He accomplished that feat against Tampa Bay in 2003, his second and final All-Star Game appearance. He can hold on to that while getting on with what he loves outside of baseball: yoga, jazz clubs, and fine restaurants.

"I can't play baseball twenty-four hours a day," Delgado told Bodley. "If I did, I'd go crazy. . . . If I'm lucky, I'll play baseball for fifteen years. Then I'm thirty-five. What am I gonna do, be a dumb jock?"

JASON GIAMBI
Oakland Athletics 1995–2001, 2009; New York Yankees 2002–2008; Colorado Rockies 2009–2012

Before Jason Giambi tumbled into baseball obscurity, he was a two-time *Sports Illustrated* cover boy.

There he was in the July 17, 2000, edition, popping off the page. Sitting on the dugout bench, elbows on knees—knees extending beyond the edges of the magazine—Giambi's gloved hands gripped the bat, which sat on his left shoulder, and he cast a blank stare from behind his shiny strands of black hair, hanging well below his nose and matching the color of the skull tattoo that covered the majority of his left deltoid and biceps.

The caption read, "Jason Giambi, Oakland slugger."

The big and bold headline: "The New Face of Baseball: How the Home Run Has Changed the Game."

The positive press didn't end there. Giambi was more than a mere personality. He had what it takes to get the attention—a combination of power and average.

Less than three years after Giambi's *Sports Illustrated* cover debut, the magazine put a different Giambi on the front, headlining him this time on the 2002 Baseball Preview edition. Now he was a New York Yankee, cleaned up and appropriately presented, more to the liking of team owner George Steinbrenner.

Instead of wearing a sleeveless T-shirt and with no baseball cap or, for that matter, any item with team insignia, this time Giambi was presented from the waist up in full Yankees uniform, finishing off the left-handed swing that garnered him this headline: "King of Swing: Why Jason Giambi Is the Perfect Modern Hitter."

That's saying a lot.

In just a few years Giambi, the 2000 Most Valuable Player, became the new millennium's Frank Thomas—a rare example of size, power, average, run production, and discernment at the plate.

And it's no surprise that he became one of the best by learning from one of the best.

"When he was [in Oakland] is when people started talking about his at bats per home run and how amazing it was," said Giambi, speaking of Mark McGwire for a *Sports Illustrated* article in July 2000. "I learned from him how important it is to wait for your pitch and, when you get it, to slam it. It's an approach where you have to be confident. You don't always want to be in a hole, 0 and 2, but you have to know, 'Hey, I can hit with two strikes.'"

When he made this comment about McGwire, Giambi was in the middle of his best season. He was the American League's starting All-Star first baseman; McGwire was his National League counterpart. The two talked multiple times a week via the phone, and Giambi went on to win the MVP Award. What a year for the two friends, not to mention the Oakland Athletics, the first team to benefit from the mentor-apprentice relationship of McGwire and Giambi.

"That's us," Giambi also said in the *Sports Illustrated* story, referring to his A's. "Sit around and wait for the three-run Jimmy Jack."

After can-openers like Ken Caminiti, investigators like George Mitchell, tell-alls like Jose Canseco, and the naked-eye test in general, it's no surprise Giambi's 6-foot-3, 240-pound frame turned out being, in part, the result of performance-enhancing drugs. Compare him to, say, Fred McGriff, who weighed about 40 pounds less, packed a similar punch, and avoided any finger pointing.

"When Jason Giambi showed up at the New York Yankees' spring-training camp in Tampa this year, he looked as if he were auditioning for a Hollywood sequel: 'Honey, I Shrunk Myself,' wrote *Newsweek*'s Mark Starr in December of 2004. "His neck seemed to have dropped several sizes, his shoulders had new slope, and his torso could no longer be described as hulking."

So how should Giambi be remembered? As the potential-filled, second-round draft pick out of California State University who hit 67 home runs total in his first three full seasons in the majors? Or the player who hit 120 combined home runs from 2001 through 2003?

In the federal grand-jury testimony that was taken in 2003 and leaked to the *San Francisco Chronicle*, Giambi admitted to having taken steroids from 2001 through 2003. The 2000 and 2001 seasons immediately drove the Yankees to sign the free agent away from Oakland at the going rate of $120 million—the sixth-highest contract in major league history.

Giambi finished first and second, respectively, in MVP voting in 2000–2001 on the strength of power and average. He recorded a combined 81 home runs and 157 RBI and hit .333 and .342. Add a league-leading 137 walks followed by 129 the next season, and Giambi was indeed Thomas-esque, the "perfect modern hitter." And for good measure, Giambi went on to win the 2002 Home Run Derby, beating crowd favorite Sammy Sosa in the finals. (Sosa, another doper, stole the show, though, by hitting 8 home runs of more than 500 feet.)

In hindsight, Giambi's talent will probably be judged as lying somewhere between baseball peasant and baseball king. The eighteen-year veteran, who hasn't played a full season since his final one with the Yankees in 2008, was able to record three 30-plus home run seasons with the Yankees after baseball began testing for steroids, a drop from his steroid years, but also an appropriate progression for a perennial up-and-coming 20 home run hitter.

ANDRES GALARRAGA

Montreal Expos 1985–1991, 2002; St. Louis Cardinals 1992; Colorado Rockies 1993–1997; Atlanta Braves 1998, 2000; Texas Rangers 2001; San Francisco Giants 2001, 2003; Anaheim Angels 2004

Tracking Andres Galarraga's career highlights on the back of a baseball card is much like connecting the dots of a jagged constellation, one like the Big Dipper.

Starting near the top, Galarraga led the majors in hits with 184 in 1988; next trace your finger down and to the right for his league-best batting average of .370 in 1993; then drag diagonally back across the surface to 1996, when he topped everyone with 47 home runs and 150 RBI. He also led the league with 140 RBI in 1997. As for strikeouts, yes, he held that honor four times as well.

Galarraga once said he stressed making hard contact rather than trying to hit homers, saying, "[I] just go for line drives." That explains the high average.

As Andre Dawson once said, "He's a guy you can make a mistake with and he can lose a ball." And that explains the 399 career home runs.

As is often the case with sluggers, therein lies Galarraga's potential for making a compelling run at the coveted and elusive Triple Crown. Midway through his nineteen-year career in 1996, Galarraga made his push with a stat line for Colorado that looked like this: .304-47-150.

Only Tony Gwynn's .353 batting average blocked Galarraga from baseball immortality. But to some extent the baseball give-and-take between the two hitters ended even steven, as Galarraga's major-league-best .370 average in 1993 kept Gwynn from starting a year early what ultimately became a stretch of four straight batting titles (1994–1997).

Galarraga may have fallen one dinger shy of the 400 club, but everything after number 315 could be rendered icing on the cake. After fourteen seasons, split among Montreal, St. Louis, Colorado, and Atlanta, Galarraga missed the 1999 campaign because of cancer. His diagnosis came as the result of a physical to examine back pain days before spring training with the Braves.

"When the doctors told me 'lymphoma,' I thought I might be dead the next day," Galarraga told *Baseball Digest* in July 2000. "I wanted to get to a phone to talk to my mother and get home to see the kids. I was so scared."

The "Big Cat," as he was known around baseball, had the "Big C," but he returned to the diamond the following season without really missing a beat. Sure, his production was down compared to his run of MVP-like numbers from 1993 through 1998 (five top-ten finishes), but he returned in All-Star form (his fifth and final mid-summer classic appearance) by eventually ending the 2000 season with a .302 batting average with 28 home runs and 100 RBI (his fifth straight 100-plus RBI season).

Bear in mind again the unlikely recipe for such a season: this was his fifteenth big league campaign and the first following a year away from the game. "I was sick all the time. I was very weak, I knew the treatments were going to help me in the long run, but they are very difficult," Galarraga told *Baseball Digest*. "I was trying to rest one afternoon when I started to dream and there was God in my dream. I knew I was going to be OK, and when I was OK I was able to help others facing this."

As it turns out, Galarraga's comeback year was also a curtain call of kinds. He left Atlanta for Texas as a free agent after that inspiring season—and joined four other teams in four years via free agency—but neither played a full season again nor approached his usual numbers before retiring in 2004.

On the other hand, his legacy had already been set in motion. "I want to be a role model," Galarraga told *Baseball Digest* during his comeback. "When I play and hit some homers, then maybe others will see. I have no problem telling anyone what happened to me. I am smiling today and happy. I want others with cancer to see that, yes, you can smile again, too."

PAUL KONERKO

Los Angeles Dodgers 1997–1998; Cincinnati Reds 1998; Chicago White Sox 1999–2012

If ever there were a baseball edition of the longtime game show *Family Feud*, it's safe to say an answer of "raving lunatic" would earn you a strike when trying to name the most popular ways to describe Paul Konerko.

Intense, gritty, gutsy—maybe, but "raving lunatic" is better suited for a boxer or a cage fighter, not a baseball player. But it's Konerko's term, his reflection of himself, and how he frames the world he engages in, so the *Daily Herald* ran with the quote in 2000 and let him flesh out his explanation.

After Konerko was prompted with the idea that he's willing to do anything for the Chicago White Sox, including play multiple positions and fill the designated hitter role, he had this to say:

> I'm not afraid of anything. One of the best things you can be called is a gamer, a guy that will fight and scratch and claw in every at bat and every play. That's how you earn respect.
>
> That's the thing that's most important to me. Do my team-mates respect me? If you have the respect of the guys you're play-ing with, the numbers are usually going to be there.

Konerko's statement proved prophetic. He had only finished one full season at the time he raved about his lunacy, and it was a modest one: .294 batting average, 24 home runs, and 81 RBI. Not bad, though, because those numbers forecast well for a twenty-three-year-old former first-round draft pick of the Los Angeles Dodgers about to enter his sec-ond full big league season.

Over the next decade, Konerko didn't become the superstar the *Daily Herald* suggested he might become in that article, but he got close. From 2000 through 2012 the White Sox first baseman cracked six All-Star Games and twice finished in the top ten for MVP voting. He also helped the White Sox end an eighty-eight-year drought by winning the 2005 World Series.

"Konerko is not a superstar, but a few other teams likely will offer him superstar money," wrote columnist Rick Morrissey for the *Chicago Tribune* sixteen days after the World Series ended. He continued,

> If I were in charge of the Sox's money (and it's only a matter of time before I am), I'd cap my offer at four years, $52 million. If

the Angels or the Red Sox want to get into a bidding war for his services, want to give him $15 million or more a year, bless them.

Konerko ended up signing a five-year, $60 million deal through 2010 and then re-signed through 2013—when he's scheduled to make $13.5 million. Konerko's best years might be ahead of him. He finished fifth in the MVP race in 2010 by hitting .312 with 39 home runs and 111 RBI, his best numbers in those categories since 2006. Or maybe 2010 was a swan song. Time will tell for the sixteen-year veteran.

Konerko has never led the league in any significant offensive category other than grounding into double plays, which he did 28 times in 2003. He twice finished as runner-up in the home run race (41 in 2004, 39 in 2010).

Numbers aside, Konerko's legacy (like that of many aging sluggers) may have been solidified in younger years. In leading the White Sox to the Promised Land in 2005, Konerko picked up the American League Championship Series MVP Award. In 5 games against the Los Angeles Angels of Anaheim, Konerko batted .286 with 2 home runs and 7 RBI to go along with a .619 slugging percentage.

"I'm not playing just to be average. And I'm not playing just to make money and get out," said Konerko before the start of the 2000 season, when he was set to make only $305,000. (In 2011, by comparison, he made $12 million.) "I want to see what I can do in this game. When I'm done playing, I'd hate to sit back and think I didn't give it my best shot."

3

DEFENSE

Playing first base is a snap, right? Consider the case of Carlos Santana, normally a catcher for Cleveland. On April 3, 2011, he was stationed at first base. In the fourth inning Carlos Quentin led off second base for the White Sox and A. J. Pierzynski took his lead from first. Alexei Ramirez popped up a bunt, which Santana stabbed after diving for the ball. He then threw to second baseman Orlando Cabrera covering first to nab Pierzynski, for the second out, and when Cabrera fired to shortstop Asdrubal Cabrera covering second base, the force-out on Quentin, who, like Pierzynski, had roamed all the way to the next base, capped an easy, leisurely triple play. What was so odd here is that the man who started the triple killing, Santana, was playing first base for the first time in the majors. Routine, eh?

Not so. Simply put, first base is not as easy a position to play as some people believe. For a large part of Stan Musial's career he stated he didn't enjoy playing first, because it was a great deal of work. He noted that "in the outfield, if the ball is hit to someone else, all you do is watch. At first base, you're jumping off on every pitch. . . . You're in on every play, more or less." He added that fielding sizzling ground balls at first base was another tough task, one he didn't have to deal with in the outfield.

Don Padgett, an occasional first baseman with the Cardinals, found himself on the bench at one point in 1937. He approached his manager, Billy Southworth, demanding to know why he wasn't playing despite his .400 average. Southworth tersely replied, "Because you're a .399 fielder." Southworth's assessment of Padgett's value to the team indicates one can't simply "hide" a good hitter at first base—not totally, not without sometimes getting hurt on the defensive side of the ledger.

Many people feel, though, that hitting is the tough part of baseball, and that diligent players should be able to become good fielders. As first baseman Adam LaRoche put it, "Your defense can be consistent—there's no excuse to screw up on defense, but hitting is going to come and go."

First base can also be a perilous position to play. Aubrey Huff spoke about the method he uses on one of the most dangerous plays a first baseman faces, when an infielder's throw takes him into the path of the batter/runner. Many times on such a play a collision ensues, sometimes body to body, other times between the runner and the arm or shoulder of the first baseman. Huff observed that it's not as simple as merely concentrating on the ball more:

> No, when you know you're going to get hit it's kind of just trying to get out of the way, depending on where the runner is. Obviously, that's an injury right there that can take you out for the season. I've seen plenty of guys put that arm out there and dislocate their shoulder or whatever. I mean, depending on the time [or circumstances] of the game and if it's a blowout, you just stay out of the way. I mean, if you're 20 games out and in last place, get out of the way. If it's playoff time or whatever, you just take it [the risk].

The risk is as real as it is palpable for the first basemen every single time he plays the position. To quote Huff again, "Oh, absolutely. A guy is coming down as hard as he can to first and that arm sticks out on a bad throw—I've seen plenty of guys get hurt that way."

First base can be a place of shame for a runner who gets picked off or runs when he shouldn't have (perhaps because he missed a sign or lost track of the number of outs). It can also be a place of humiliation for a slow batter/runner who is thrown out by an aggressive right fielder with a strong arm. Then there was the case of Sean Casey, who took part in one of the strangest plays ever involving a man being thrown out at first base. The key here is *how* or from *where* he was thrown out.

The peculiar play took place during the Chicago White Sox at Detroit Tigers game of August 24, 2006, when an old baseball paradox was proven. "If you stick around the game long enough, you'll see it all, yet even if you watch baseball forever, you'll still see something new."

Tigers first baseman Casey hit what was apparently a clean single, a hard line drive that shot into left field, but he was still gunned out at first by the *left fielder*.

Detroit pitcher Nate Robertson, who was there that day, explained,

> We were playing the White Sox and Sean Casey hit a line drive that appeared to him that [Chicago White Sox third baseman] Joe Crede had jumped up and caught. Well, it actually ended up going off the top of his glove. Sean "saw" it in his glove and started walking back to the dugout.

Casey was certain the ball had nestled into Crede's webbing after he saw Crede momentarily glance into his glove. However, Crede was merely inspecting the mitt, perhaps to see if the webbing had come loose. That action lulled Casey, who gave up on the play after taking about three strides down the first base line.

Robertson continued, "The ball went to left field where Pablo Ozuna ended up coming in and picking it up as Sean realized that the ball cleared the glove, and he got thrown out at first base from left field."

Even though Casey was normally an all-out guy, the moment he headed back toward his dugout, he was doomed. When he finally realized the ball was alive and in play, he began his mad dash for first base, but it was too late—the hustling Ozuna had fielded the ball in short left field and had rifled a one-bounce throw to first base to retire a shocked Casey on a bang-bang play. As Casey himself later noted, he had been blessed with many baseball assets, "but speed wasn't one of them."

Later, on the MLB network's show *Quick Pitch*, he said that as he was trying to beat the play to avoid becoming what may well be the only big league player to ever get thrown out from left field on a "hit," he felt as if he were "running in quicksand." As he ran, this thought crossed his mind, inducing a sense of panic: "Please don't get thrown out from left field."

After the play he asked first base umpire Ron Colpa, "If there was one call you could have blown, couldn't you blow that one for me?"

While first base was a venue of humiliation for Casey, others have tried to find peace there. Toward the end of his career, catcher Mike Piazza, like many aging players, sought to finish his career in a less demanding position. He soon learned the move to first was not such an easy one—he would last just 68 games there in 2004 before giving up the experiment, never again to play that position.

Former big leaguer Kevin Rhomberg had this to say about players who shift from another position to first base and the demands of playing there:

> I was a utility guy. I played some outfield and some infield and I was a back-up first baseman as well. It's a great place to play. You're almost like the catcher, you're in there on almost every play, every ground ball you've got to do something, and you're the cutoff to [plays at home], you've got relays, you cover bunts. I mean, first base is a place where all the good athletes can go and do well at the end of their career or [when they] need to slide over there. When you get there, you really enjoy it.

Still, Rhomberg added that the position can be tough on a newcomer. "It's not only how difficult, but learning the position—you have more than just your responsibility. There's covering bunts; and PFP [pitchers' fielding practice] with the pitchers is a lot of extra work, too."

Rhomberg said that even veteran first basemen sometimes make an easy play more difficult than it should be:

> The play that still gets me at first base is if you have a runner on first, or first and second, or bases loaded and there are two outs. When the first baseman gets a ground ball, even if it's to your right, they get it, they stop, they turn, and they hit the

pitcher on the run at first base. With two outs all you've got to do is flip it to second. You don't see enough of this, especially at the amateur level—it's so easy. "Hey, on a ball hit to my right, I'm coming to you at shortstop." It's easier than trying to hit the pitcher on the run to beat the base runner.

Another catcher, Hall of Famer Johnny Bench, said that his move to first was a drastic one because the "level of looking at things from two and a half feet off the ground to six feet—it's a different perspective." In short, not everyone can handle the chores at first base.

That said, playing first base is easier than playing positions such as shortstop and catcher. Too, not all players are content to man the *relatively* easy position. Al Oliver broke in with the Pittsburgh Pirates in 1968. By 1974, when he had roamed the outfield for the Bucs in more than 400 contests, he had come to believe the outfield belonged to him. He had been the starting first baseman in 1969. Two years later he was asked to spend much more time in the outfield after speedy Matty Alou was traded to the St. Louis Cardinals. Oliver quickly grew accustomed to, and fond of, the outfield. So when the Pirates asked him to return to first base in 1974, rewarding him for his toil in 1973 with what Pittsburgh writer Charley Feeney called "a large pay boost to $80,000," Oliver griped that he didn't want to play first base.

Just as Musial felt playing the outfield afforded him more time to think about his hitting, Oliver contended that moving to first could hamper his offensive game. Aside from playing 56 more games at first, he spent the rest of his days with the Pirates as an outfielder, and hit .308 or higher in three of those four seasons.

Having covered some of the greatest slugging first basemen ever, it's time now to zero in on the best players ever to handle that position with defensive wizardry.

One way to measure fielding skill is to take into consideration winners of the Gold Glove Award. The awards were first presented in 1957 by Rawlings, a maker of sporting goods. The winners are determined annually by the voting done by managers and coaches with the stipulation that they cannot cast a vote for a player from their team. The voters are also limited to selecting players from their own league.

Using this award as an indication of defensive ability has a vital caveat attached to it in that winning a Gold Glove does not mean the player was, in fact, the best defensive man at his position. Some critics point out that winners who are also good hitters get a break over those who aren't as well known for their offensive output.

Additionally, there have been glaring errors in the voting. In 1999, for example, Rafael Palmeiro, a man who led his league in assists five times, won his third straight Gold Glove for his play at first base—this time copping the award on reputation and his offensive output, not for his defensive skills. Amazingly, the voters ignored (or were unaware of) the fact that he had played a mere 28 games at first that year (he had served as the Rangers designated hitter in 135 games). Some experts felt Palmeiro's replacement, Lee Stevens (133 games at first with a .994 fielding percentage), deserved the honor. No doubt Palmeiro was actually being honored for his offense, not defense. That season he put up personal bests for homers (47), runs driven in (148), and batting average (.324).

While Joe Charboneau, the AL Rookie of the Year in 1980, felt that hitting standout Rod Carew was actually one of the best defensive first basemen around during the early 1980s, he observed that some great gloves weren't big name stars. "The kid the White Sox had, Mike Squires, he had great hands—best defensive first baseman [I saw]. They'd bring him in for defense. Fabulous first baseman. And John Wockenfuss with Detroit was pretty good."

Even with the understanding that the Mike Squires of the baseball world tend to be ignored when it comes to passing out awards, taking a look at the list of the first basemen who have won multiple Gold Gloves through 2012 is still worthwhile: Keith Hernandez, eleven times; Don Mattingly, nine; George Scott, eight; Vic Power and Bill White, seven; Wes Parker and J. T. Snow, six; Mark Teixeira, five; Steve Garvey, Mark Grace, four; Adrian Gonzalez, Todd Helton, Gil Hodges, Eddie Murray, John Olerud, Rafael Palmeiro, Joe Pepitone, and Derrek Lee, three; Cecil Cooper, Andres Galarraga, Jim Spencer, and Albert Pujols, two.

Others who played before the award was first presented may be overlooked by today's fans, but they deserve respect. Mike Humeston, a baseball scout who has been around the game for many years, pointed out that one of the best gloves he ever saw at first base was George

McQuinn, who played primarily with the St. Louis Browns. Humeston's assessment: "Soft hands, very good [fielder]."

Walter Johnson claimed that the greatest fielding first baseman of his era was Hal Chase. Known as Prince Hal, he was great with the glove but hardly princely in the honesty department, and is believed to have bet on his opponents and then thrown big league games. When Christy Mathewson managed Chase in 1918 he became the third manager to accuse Chase of throwing games. Mathewson suspended Chase for two months for corruption. The next year the president of the National League banned Chase from baseball on further charges of throwing games. Later on, evidence implicated Chase in the fixing of the 1919 World Series, arguably baseball's biggest blemish, when the Chicago White Sox rigged the Fall Classic. Chase is said to have won $40,000 betting on those games.

Over the years first basemen have worked endlessly to improve their work with the glove. When Gregg Jefferies, a versatile player who spent 275-plus games at second, third, outfield, and first base over his fourteen big league seasons, was young, he practiced diligently with his father. One drill, taking hot grounders off cement surfaces, was devised to re-create the way ground balls skid on artificial turf. "My dad would tape up balls with black electrician tape and it would kind of skip like you were on turf."

What works for one first baseman might not work for another but, one thing's for certain—players will stick with their methods as long as they're producing positive results. Here, then, are capsule comments on some of the men who mastered defensive play at first and plied their trade there as the best of the best.

FRANK CHANCE
Chicago Orphans 1898–1902, 1903–1912; New York Yankees 1913–1914

Frank Chance is a Hall of Famer who is forgotten today by most fans, except as a part of the famed Chicago Cubs double play combination of legend, [Joe] Tinker-to-[Johnny] Evers-to-Chance, remembered by those with some knowledge of this man. Chance was mainly considered to be a good defensive first baseman, even though he hit a solid .298 for his career and twice led his league in fielding percentage.

Later he was no slouch as a manager. Nicknamed the Peerless Leader, he won 116 contests with his 1916 Cubs, still a major league zenith, and his troops won four pennants over a five-year span from 1906 through 1910. In fact, as a player-manager, he won three pennants and a World Series in his first three full seasons he held those titles. He then finished in second place before winning yet another pennant.

Chance also gained trivia immortality when he became the first player ever tossed from a World Series game back in the 1910 Series.

STEVE GARVEY

A player cannot be accurately judged for his defensive play solely by considering stats such as fielding percentage and total errors. For instance, a generous home official scorer can aid a player, as can a first baseman's lack of range—a man can't commit an error on balls he can't get to. While not as good as Keith Hernandez, Garvey, who gained most of his fame with the Los Angeles Dodgers, deserves recognition for his .999 fielding percentage in 1981, tied then as the best ever, and for having topped that with an unblemished 1.000 percentage in 1984. Upon his retirement he held the record for the best lifetime fielding percentage as well, .996, and for the fewest errors in a season.

Garvey attributed his good footwork and his quickness around the bag to his football roots—he was a defensive back at Michigan State University.

KEVIN YOUKILIS
Boston Red Sox 2004–2012; Chicago White Sox 2012

CASEY KOTCHMAN
Anaheim Angels 2004; Los Angeles Angels of Anaheim 2005–2008; Atlanta Braves 2008–2009; Boston Red Sox 2009; Seattle Mariners 2010; Tampa Bay Rays 2011; Cleveland Indians 2012

From the Fourth of July 2006 through June 6, 2008, Kevin Youkilis of the Red Sox played errorless ball at first base, establishing a new record by accepting 2,002 chances without a miscue, well beyond the former record of 1,700 errorless chances. That streak, because first base is easier to play than other positions, is by far the longest for any position. The closest such streak had been 1,565 by catcher Mike Matheny. In all, Youkilis went a record 238 games between errors, topping the old mark held by Steve Garvey.

However, Casey Kotchman, with the Cleveland Indians in 2012, overtook the record for consecutive errorless games. His defensive run lasted exactly two years and two months from June 20, 2008, until August 21, 2010 (274 games). Only Youkilis and Kotchman ever put up errorless stretches of 200-plus games, and both have a chance to wind up with the record for the highest fielding percentage. Through 2012, as a matter of fact, Kotchman's career fielding percentage stood at .9977 to Youkilis's .9974, the best two marks ever.

VIC POWER

Philadelphia Athletics 1954; Kansas City 1955–1958; Cleveland Indians 1958–1961; Minnesota Twins 1962–1964; Los Angeles Angels 1964; Philadelphia Phillies 1964; California Angels 1965

Power, as smooth as aloe vera lotion, won the first seven Gold Gloves handed out in the American League. Power played from 1954 through 1965 and won that award in virtually every season that he could feasibly do so: the award was not given out during his first three seasons. The following year only one award was presented for both leagues— Gil Hodges won it. And Power failed to win a Gold Glove in his final season, with the California Angels—but every other season he did take home the Gold Glove hardware. He even won the award in the AL during his next-to-last season, even though he played in only 60 games for the Angels and the Minnesota Twins. Power is also one of a handful of men to win this honor with three different clubs. Moreover, on six occasions he led his league in assists by a first baseman. He fielded hot smashes with the deft hands and precision of a surgeon, and he is recognized, to this day, as one of the best fielders ever at his position.

One of the most interesting tales involving Power involves his lack of base-stealing ability—he stole only 45 lifetime bases with a season high of just 9. Despite that, in August 1958 he stole home twice in the same game. However, for the entire season he wound up with just one additional stolen base.

Longtime scout Mike Humeston, who called Power "one of the best gloves ever: flashy, soft hands," had a friend, Steve Jankowski, who played with Power in the minors, mainly as a second baseman. Humeston recalled Jankowski telling him that Power reassured infielders to "just throw the ball over by the bag, I'll be there to make the play."

BILL WHITE
New York Giants 1956; San Francisco Giants 1958; St. Louis Cardinals 1959–1965, 1969; Philadelphia Phillies 1966–1968

Winning seven Gold Gloves says a lot, and White, who played for the Giants, Cardinals, and Phillies, and who would go on to become the NL president, was a force on both sides of the ball. He hit 202 homers while maintaining a .286 batting average. A member of eight All-Star squads, his Gold Gloves came in successive years, 1960–1966. In 1956 he led the NL in both putouts and assists. His biggest playing thrill, though, had to be when his Cardinals won the 1964 World Series.

GEORGE SISLER
St. Louis Browns 1915–1922, 1924–1927; Washington Senators 1928; Boston Braves 1928–1930

George Sisler is best known for his batting prowess, but he was a multidimensional player. On May 1, 1912, when he was nineteen years old, three years before his big league career began with the St. Louis Browns, he pitched for the University of Michigan and dazzled the opposition. The freshman southpaw worked seven innings, striking out 20 batters to account for all but one out single-handedly.

In the majors, Sisler, who hit over .400 twice—with a personal best of .420 in 1922, the third greatest average of the modern era—set a record in 1920 for the most hits ever in a season (257). That record stood until Ichiro Suzuki collected 262 hits in 2004, doing so in 70 more plate appearances than Sisler while playing over a 162-game schedule to Sisler's 154-game season. By the way, in 1922 Sisler enjoyed a torrid 41-game hitting streak, one of the longest ever. Surprisingly, though, it wasn't all that torrid of a streak because during the span he hit .421, a mere one point better than what he would hit for the entire season.

The argument here is that baseball's record book should include two lists: one for the greatest feats established over the old 154-game schedule and one for those set since the baseball season was expanded by 8 games. Under these guidelines, in 1961, when Roger Maris eclipsed Babe Ruth's venerated record for the most homers in a season, baseball would not have been involved in any controversy concerning the placing of an asterisk next to Maris's 61 homers; baseball's two-columned record book would have honored both Maris and Ruth (the latter with his 60 home runs, amassed over a shorter schedule). After all, why punish a player such as Ruth or Sisler for something they had no control over?

As for defense, *Sports Illustrated* named Sisler as the second-best defensive first baseman ever, calling him "quick and agile" and possessing perhaps the best arm ever at his position. Sisler actually led his league in first base assists six times.

Incidentally, Sisler's son, Dick, also a first baseman, was a lightweight hitter compared to his father, hitting .276 lifetime and never topping .300 in a single season, let alone .400, but he did one thing few men ever accomplish. On the final day of the 1950 season his game-winning home run in the tenth inning clinched a pennant for the Phillies "Whiz Kids," their first flag in thirty-five years.

TODD HELTON
Colorado Rockies 1997–2012

When Todd Helton, a great fielder for the Colorado Rockies who topped the NL in assists four times, was asked what defensive play was the toughest one for him to execute, he said, somewhat surprisingly, that it was fielding pop-ups. When asked if it was because they often twist toward the foul line or because he has to sometimes fight the sun or fans for the ball, he replied with a chuckle, "It's because I'm no good at it." His solution: "I just keep taking them [in practice]."

The three-time Gold Glove winner added that charging bunts, then firing to second for the force play, is a difficult play because it requires a split-second, crucial decision, one made more difficult because "you can't even see the runner."

His third choice for the most demanding play was holding a runner on first, then coming off the bag with the pitch, only to have to field a ball headed crisply back toward the foul line. Without the proper foot-work, he said, making the catch is impossible—one's feet must be planted as the pitch crosses the plate.

Some plays that fans might feel are difficult, such as when a fielder must decide if he has time to make a throw to the plate to nail a runner or whether he should take a sure out; or whether to try to make the throw to second base to start a tough double play or simply take an easy out at first base, are not challenging to Helton.

> It's just like Little League—you know what you're going to do
> with the ball before it's hit to you. That's what you ask yourself.
> Everything is thought out. A fielder has to know the speed of
> the runners involved, the score at the time, he has to gauge how
> hard the ball has been hit so he can factor in how much time
> he has to make a play, and so on.

Helton has been known to range almost into third basemen's ter-ritory to field bunts, which is a rare ability among first basemen.

When asked what baseball skill he is most proud of, he indicated it was playing defense in general. "I think defense is something that anybody can be good at if they work hard enough, and hopefully I'm working hard enough to be a halfway decent first baseman," he said with modesty during a 2003 interview. At that time he was coming off two successive seasons in which he took home the NL Gold Glove Award.

One way he tried to improve was by working on facets of his game when he took infield (practiced his defense):

I do it all the time. Every day there's something I work on, something different. Whether it's going to the right, or now I'm working on using one hand, being more relaxed with my glove hand so it's not stiff. At lot of times I get two hands down there and I get stiff, so I hold a ball in [my left] hand now so I don't use [my right] hand.

Helton said that from time to time he tended to catch himself slipping into, say, a bad habit defensively, and he would then work on getting back on track in that respect.

Helton also talked about those of his peers whose skills he respects: Mark Grace, J. T. Snow, Andres Galarraga, and Derrek Lee.

No slouch at the plate, this former college quarterback at Tennessee (he played there from 1993 through 1994 between the tenure of two other key quarterbacks for the Vols, Heath Shuler and Peyton Manning) posted a single season best batting average of a lusty .372 in 2000 when he flirted with the .400 plateau into the month of September. That season he led the league in a slew of categories, including total bases (405), doubles (59), and RBI (147—he followed that total up with an additional 146 the next season).

From 2000 through 2009 no major leaguer had more than Helton's 431 doubles. He also had the third-highest batting average over that period (.331) and the second-best on-base percentage (.436), which was a distant 81 points behind the number of the suspiciously bulked up Barry Bonds. Helton's lifetime batting average of .320 is the fifty-third highest ever.

JEFF BAGWELL

Jeff Bagwell has one Gold Glove (1994) to his credit and has led the NL in assists by a first baseman on five occasions. He broke down some of the key ingredients a first baseman needs to succeed. "Footwork is very important—it's the one thing that's very hard to get in the beginning. I guess it's the most important thing. After that," he joked, "it's pretty much just catching the baseball. It sounds easy, but at times it's not and there are a lot of things you can do to help your infielders—scooping the ball and the way you stretch."

However, Bagwell believes the concept of the large first baseman's mitts helping on scoops

is a fallacy—I'm not so sure it's the mitt. More than anything else, you're either good at it, or you're not. Now you can do some things [to improve]—you can have some guy stand 20 feet away from you and throw the ball in the dirt. Although that's a different angle a lot of times than the normal one, [it's the] repetition. Just getting to see as many balls as you can to know how the ball's going to react off the dirt.

Low throws also come whistling over to first from pitchers on pick-off attempts. Interestingly, not all pitchers are the same on their throws to the bag.

Octavio Dotel has a tough time throwing to first base—I don't like when he throws over because I have no idea where it's going to go. There are guys that are very easy [to catch] then, after you watch them for a while you know when they're going to throw over so it's no big deal. It depends, too. You could be out here in Cincinnati today and you got fifty white shirts behind you—it's tough to see the ball. More than anything else, it's just seeing the ball from the pitcher—that's the hardest part about it.

Bagwell agreed that there is much more to playing first than most fans realize. Take the playing surface, for instance. "Different cuts in the grass and different surface—there's some bad dirt out there, Atlanta's awful and Chicago's not the greatest. Other places are great and you feel very comfortable in those. You get around enough, you understand that." So when Bagwell's playing in, say, Atlanta, his attitude becomes a sort of "I've got to sacrifice my body more. I'll smother the ball if necessary." He put it this way: "You just have to be able to realize there are going to be some bad hops so you better get in front of the ball."

Born in Boston and drafted by the Red Sox in the fourth round of the 1989 June Amateur Draft, he began his pro career as a third baseman. However, with Wade Boggs, who won five batting titles over a six-year span (1983–1988), playing third for the parent Red Sox club, Bagwell was expendable. Late in 1990 they shipped him to Houston in a fiasco of a trade for Larry Andersen, who would pitch just 22 innings for the Red Sox before moving on to San Diego the following season.

Bagwell felt that the key to his transition to first base with Houston was

> the footwork getting to the bag while the ball is being thrown. At third base your glove hand has more plays and at first base it's your back hand. So I had to work a lot harder on my back hand once I got to the big leagues at first base because that's where more of your balls are [hit to a right-handed throwing first-sacker].

Perhaps surprising to many fans, Bagwell said that, like Helton, he felt that over his career his biggest weakness in the field was "probably pop-ups, too." During a 2003 interview, when he was thirty-five years old, he stated,

> Now it's probably range because I'm getting older, but pop-ups are difficult at times just because of the sun, you're going backward, and when you're on a corner you're going toward the stands or the dugout, and things like that. They're very easy when I'm in our place [in Houston], which has a closed roof.

JOHN OLERUD

Toronto Blue Jays 1989–1996; New York Mets 1997–1999; Seattle Mariners 2000–2004; New York Yankees 2004; Boston Red Sox 2005

Winner of three Gold Gloves, all with Seattle, Olerud was a vital part of the 1999 New York Mets infield that won two Gold Gloves, both on the left side of the infield. Although he didn't win a Gold Glove that season, he saved countless errors for teammates with his stretching and scooping skills. The four-man unit, which included Robin Ventura at third, Rey Ordonez at short, second baseman Edgardo Alfonzo, and Olerud, blanketed the infield like a 10-inch-deep snowfall and established a major league record for the fewest errors in a season, a minuscule 27, by an infield. Overall, this airtight group of players posted a fielding percentage of .992 and gave up only 20 unearned runs all year long.

Olerud, who hit a personal high of .363 when he won a batting title in 1993, said the most difficult defensive play for him was handling a throw on the in-between hop. "It's not far away enough where you can read the hop and it's not close enough that you can smother it. You're kind of at the mercy of what kind of hop it's going to take." On such plays he tended to try to backhand the ball while attempting "to keep as much [of the mitt's] pocket showing as I can."

Olerud, as affable as he is classy, almost didn't get the opportunity to play major league ball—he nearly died when he was in college. On January 11, 1989, after he had finished working out with his Washington State University baseball team, he collapsed. He was rushed to a doctor who diagnosed Olerud with a subarachnoid hemorrhage, brought on by bleeding from a blood vessel at the base of his brain. Unaware of his surroundings and in bad shape, he was medevacked to a medical complex. Doctors there wondered if Olerud's situation might be like that of basketball star Hank Gathers, who died of a heart problem, or that he might have meningitis, an aneurysm, or a brain tumor.

Eventually doctors detected an aneurysm that they repaired over the course of a six-hour surgery. In order to clip the aneurysm doctors had to remove "a window of bone" from Olerud's skull.

It took two weeks before he was well enough to return to his own bed and four weeks before he recovered enough to return to light workouts with his team. Olerud's father, Dr. John E. Olerud, who had been a catcher in the minors, said that it is unusual for a person to undergo aneurysm surgery and then go on to play professional baseball, calling his son's recovery and ascension to the majors a miracle.

Throughout his playing days Olerud wore a protective helmet, even when playing the field, and a visible dent is still present on the side of his head.

MARK GRACE

In a 1996 piece, *Sports Illustrated* named Mark Grace the best active defensive first baseman, citing his great range and hands. Upon his retirement, he had recorded the second- and third-highest single season assist totals and had the fourth-most lifetime assists by a first baseman. Although he led the NL in errors during his rookie year with a humiliating total of 18 misplays, he quickly improved and by 1991 began a three-year stretch in which he led the league in both assists and putouts by a first-sacker. In 1992 his .998 fielding percentage was the best ever by a Cubs first baseman. Even near the end of his career, in 2000 at the age of thirty-six, he was still adept enough to lead the league in fielding percentage.

When he was with the Diamondbacks he gave his thoughts on fielding and the main attributes needed to play first base:

> Obviously you got to practice it and you got to work at it. You got to have instincts; you have to have a feel for the game. You got to know who your hitter is, who your base runners are, who your pitcher is—is he an off speed guy, is the left-hander going to be pulling the ball my way? That sort of song and dance.
>
> You just have to be around awhile before you can become a "Gold Glove–caliber [fielder]." You have to have the experience of different fields—is it a fast surface, is it a slower surface? Like at Wrigley Field [in Chicago], it was a slow surface. I mean, you could hide small animals in the infield grass.
>
> And it's just being prepared. OK, if the ball's hit to me, where am I going with it, what do I want to do with it? Just playing it out in your mind before the situation happens.

Young fielders must learn, for instance, how far they can range to their right before it's actually wiser to put on the brakes and let the second baseman make a more routine play on the ball. Grace noted,

> I don't think you ever really learn that. The only thing you have to do is just be aware of where your second baseman is. That's

what I tell my second basemen: "Hey, I'm over in the hole, you can move up the middle." Or, "Hey, I'm on the line, you're going to have to get some balls over here." You got to communicate and be talking out there.

In a 2003 interview Grace said,

When Jay Bell was a second baseman here [with the Arizona Diamondbacks], I probably talked to him more in one year than I ever talked to Ryno [Ryne Sandberg, Cubs great] in eleven years. He just wasn't a very talkative guy. So the first year I'm here [in Arizona], I'm like, "Wow, I got a second baseman that wants to talk to me." Ryno was one of the best to ever play the game, but you didn't even know he was out there if you didn't see him.

Another factor first basemen must consider is the amount of range a second baseman has. That will help determine how far a first baseman must roam to his right. According to Grace,

if you've got a guy that doesn't have much range, you have to play a little more in the hole. If you've got a guy like a Junior Spivey or Matt Kata, guys who can really get over, you can take a [step or two more to the left], take away a few more doubles down the right field line. So, it's obviously valuable to have [teammates] with a lot of range.

Often a team will put on a drastic infield shift against dead pull hitters such as Jim Thome or Ryan Howard. Grace was asked if such a hitter began tiring down the stretch run or if he were in a prolonged slump, would he and his fellow infielders stop putting on the shift and show a different defense? He reflected,

Not that I know of. If you're going to play him like that once, you're usually going to play him like that—that's the way you're going to play him that year. So, you just go by his charts [showing his hitting tendencies]. You got scouting that says where he's

hitting his ground balls and we pretty much have meetings and
know where to play guys.

Grace concluded by noting that the great fielders, the special ones,
are not only confident and prepared,

> they weren't afraid to have the ball hit to them in a big situation,
> and that's something you've got to overcome—the fear. You've
> got to want the baseball. That's my biggest dream: bases loaded,
> two outs, seventh game of the World Series, and the ball hit to
> me. That's the dream you want.

He added that not everyone shares that dream and that "a lot of
people have that anxiety" and *don't* want the ball hit their way in a tense
situation.

DARIN ERSTAD

*California Angels 1996; Anaheim Angels 1997–2004; Los Angeles
Angels of Anaheim 2005–2006; Chicago White Sox 2007; Houston
Astros 2008–2009*

Darin Erstad played 887 big league games in the outfield to 627 at first,
mainly with the Angels, and said he preferred the outfield. He found
the toughest part of his move to first was "the different throwing
motion, shortening it up and being accurate to the bases—just something you really don't do; in the outfield you can close your eyes and
throw it to the base, in the infield it's a little tougher."

Many of the other plays, such as ones involving pitchers covering
first, taking a toss from the first baseman, is something "you just get
used to doing. That's just repetition—pretty much everything is repetition, but most of those plays are reaction plays and you make good
flips to him. You just have to use your instincts as much as you can."
Erstad even felt knowing how far to range to his right before giving
way to the second baseman was routine. "Just play, whatever happens,
happens. You can't start thinking about things too much out there."

The man could hit, too. As early as June 10, 2000, Erstad banged out his 100th hit of the season, making him the fastest man to reach that level since 1934, when Heinie Manush did it in 60 games. Erstad maintained a hot clip and wound up with a league leading 240 hits, the thirteenth-highest total in baseball history. He ended the year with a glittering .355 batting average.

Not only could Erstad handle a bat and glove, he was also familiar with the pigskin. He was a member of the University of Nebraska football team that won the national championship in 1994 under coach Tom Osborne. Erstad, a punter and place kicker who had drilled a 50-yard field goal once in high school, spent only one season with Nebraska, deciding to concentrate instead on baseball. Cornhusker fans still fondly remember his key showing in the 24–17 Orange Bowl win over Miami to clinch the national title.

As a baseball player he did something rare—he won Gold Gloves for his play both in the outfield and at first base. In fact, when he won the award as a first baseman in 2004 it was only the second season he played at that spot in 80 or more games. His relative inexperience there didn't stop him from being recognized for his fine glove work.

Men such as Helton and Erstad are not unique in having played both football and baseball. Jim Thorpe and George Halas, much more famous for their football connection, also played pro baseball. An injury shut down Halas as a baseball player in 1919—he lasted just 12 games as a Yankees outfielder and was replaced in right field by none other than Babe Ruth.

Lou Gehrig also played fullback as a collegian at Columbia, and famed pitcher Christy Mathewson was a kicker at Bucknell. Another man who played some first base in the majors, Mickey Hatcher, was a punter and receiver on Oklahoma's 1977 Fiesta Bowl squad. College ball aside, in the twentieth century just over sixty men played professionally in both football and baseball.

GIL HODGES

Brooklyn Dodgers 1943, 1947–1957; Los Angeles Dodgers 1958–1961; New York Mets 1962–1963

When Casey Stengel managed an aging Gil Hodges of the New York Mets, the Old Professor observed, "He fields better on one leg than anybody else I got on two."

Later Hodges would go on to become the skipper of the 1969 Miracle Mets, a team that shocked the baseball world, winning the World Series over the Orioles.

The eight-time All-Star ended his career with 370 homers, 310 of which came in the glorious 1950s, a period in which his Dodgers won five pennants and finished in second place three other times. Further, 4 of his 310 homers in that decade came in a single game. An All-Star eight times, Hodges could slug and field—he took home three Gold Gloves.

J. T. SNOW

New York Yankees 1992; California Angels 1993–1996; San Francisco Giants 1997–2005, 2008; Boston Red Sox 2006

Snow's work with the leather was as smooth as jazz and as consistent as iambic pentameter. After all, they don't hand out six Gold Gloves to defensive dabblers.

When asked to name a standout first baseman, the first name that came to the mind of former big league pitcher Mike Koplove was lefty J. T. Snow. "He's obviously a great first baseman. It's his hands and experience [that made him stand out]. The guys at this level, especially the better defensive players, know where to position themselves. They have a knack for knowing what pitch is coming and leaning kind of that way." Snow, said Koplove, had the ability to anticipate where a pitch would be hit.

> You know, on a breaking ball, playing the guy to pull, or on a fastball—you can kind of read it, the path of the ball when it's

in the air from the pitcher's hand, and kind of get a feel for where the ball's going to be hit. I think the better defensive players can do that.

Jeff Bagwell called Snow "great, probably the best I've seen. He does everything well—turns the double play well, makes all the picks [scoops], he's got a good arm, accurate arm."

Accolades also came from former teammate Darin Erstad, who said simply, "There's nobody that's any better than he is. He's got the whole package. I mean, if you're going to have anybody watch and learn how to play that position, you just tell them to watch video of him."

Snow apparently inherited his good hands from his father, Jack, a wide receiver for the Los Angeles Rams by way of Notre Dame. Jack once led the NFL with an average of 26.3 yards per reception. That same season he was named to the Pro Bowl (1967). As for his son, he compiled a highly laudable lifetime fielding percentage of .995.

SCOTT SPIEZIO
Oakland Athletics 1996–1999; Anaheim Angels 2000–2003; Seattle Mariners 2004–2005; St. Louis Cardinals 2006–2007

Scott Spiezio is probably best remembered for his three-run homer in the sixth game of the 2002 World Series, a blast that helped spur his Angels on to a comeback win over the Giants and ultimately go on to capture the Series title. However, there is more to the dependable Scott Spiezio, a man who possessed great defensive tools. By the time he was in just his third full major league season, then with the Oakland A's, one of his coaches, Alfredo Griffin, told him he had the best hands on the ball club. Day in and day out, perhaps his primary value to his teams was his glove work.

As a youth Scott often trained with his father, Ed, a former big league infielder. Ed hit tennis balls to his son from an early age because, he related, they "gave [him] much quicker hops, unbelievably quicker hops [to field]. I felt if he could catch them, he could catch any ball, plus if he got hit, it wouldn't hurt him. I think that's what really helped him a lot. I used to hit rockets with tennis balls."

Scott's mother helped turn double plays with her son, and when his sisters, Deborah and Suzanne, practiced their tennis, they would work on their serves and ground strokes, driving them to the other side of the net where Scott worked on his hands, trying to catch their shots off short and long hops. Years later he would lead the AL in fielding percentage at first base with .990 and .997 marks in 2001 and 2002, respectively.

Scott, a member of a garage band, Sand Fox, was versatile enough to play almost anywhere on the diamond over his twelve seasons in the majors. He played every infield position except shortstop, played left and right field, and even appeared in one game as a pitcher, where he faced four batters, retiring three and walking one.

MARK TEIXEIRA

Through 2012 Teixeira had collected five Gold Glove Awards, more than any other active first baseman. His Yankees teammates, such as Derek Jeter, sing the praises of "Tex," a true star who not only came in second in the 2009 MVP voting, but also won both a Silver Slugger and a Gold Glove Award that season. Like Grace, early in his career Teixeira led his league in errors but went on to top the AL in putouts and fielding percentage twice after that.

ADRIAN GONZALEZ
Texas Rangers 2004–2005; San Diego Padres 2006–2010; Boston Red Sox 2011–2012; Los Angeles Dodgers 2012

Just thirty years old at the end of the 2012 season, Gonzalez had already led his league in assists twice, and the Red Sox, having acquired him in a December 2010 trade, were salivating at the prospect of having him man first base in 2011. He didn't disappoint the Boston organization or fans as he again led the league in assists that season.

Aside from being a good glove, Gonzalez piled up 161 home runs in his five years with San Diego, a total just 2 shy of the franchise's all-time best set by another first baseman, Nate Colbert, who required a period of six seasons to establish the record. Gonzalez was the type of player who was off and running (and swatting and fielding well) from season one. He hit 24 homers as a rookie and elevated those totals to 30, 36, and 40 over the following three seasons.

DERREK LEE

San Diego Padres 1997; Florida Marlins 1998–2003; Chicago Cubs 2004–2010; Atlanta Braves 2010; Baltimore Orioles 2011; Pittsburgh Pirates 2012

This two-time NL leader in assists is also a three-time Gold Glover. In 2002, with the Florida Marlins, and in 2004 and 2005, with the Chicago Cubs, he led the league in games played among all first basemen, but an injury that took place at his position in 2006 limited him to 60 games played. Manning first base can be risky and one of the most dangerous plays, stretching into the path of a runner to take a throw, put Lee on the disabled list that season with a fractured wrist.

While Bagwell called Snow the best, he also pointed out that "left-handed and right-handed first basemen are very different," and tipped his cap to Lee as a great right-handed fielder.

KENDRYS MORALES

Los Angeles Angels of Anaheim 2006–2012

In his first full season, 2009, Kendrys Morales was the leader in a little-known stat called Ultimate Zone Rating, which evaluates each time a ball enters a zone of the field manned by a given player, rating that man on his ability to get an out as measured against the norm for his position.

Experts feel Morales is one exciting player worth keeping an eye on—if he can stay healthy, that is. He was involved in one of baseball's more unusual injuries in 2010—truly a strange tale. On May 29 he hit a tenth-inning walk-off grand slam, and as normally happens when a hero provides a dramatic conclusion to a game, he was mobbed at home plate by delighted teammates. This time the celebration was short-lived, ending on a somber note when Morales went down in a heap and actually broke his left leg in the melee. His team, usually a contender, won only one game above .500 over the rest of the season (56–55), and a whopping nine men were required to replace Morales at first base.

While he did return to the team in 2011, a problem relating to the injury resurfaced and he was told that he would require additional surgery on his left ankle to remove scar tissue and debris. Worse, he was informed his season was over without him getting so much as one at bat for the year.

Offensively, Morales rebounded in 2012, insofar as he recorded 484 at bats, but he played only 28 games at first base behind two-time Gold Glove winner Albert Pujols.

ALBERT PUJOLS

More and more tools are being used in baseball to quantify performances, even on defense. In 2009 Albert Pujols not only won the NL MVP and led the league in many offensive categories, he was also tops in one of the newer defensive stats, runs saved. That statistic measures many factors such as range and the capability of a fielder to "turn a batted ball into an out." Another indication that he was no longer being regarded simply for his stick also came in 2009, when he set the all-time single season record for the most assists by a first baseman (185). The following season, when he won his second Gold Glove, his 157 assists ranked eighth all-time.

KEITH HERNANDEZ
St. Louis Cardinals 1974–1983; New York Mets 1983–1989; Cleveland Indians 1990

In 1999, an elite group of thirteen baseball experts surveyed by *USA Today* came up with their All-Glove team for the previous twenty-five years, focusing on men who spent most of their playing days from 1974 on. Hernandez, who won eleven Gold Gloves, all consecutive (1978–1988) over his seventeen-year career spent primarily with the New York Mets and the St. Louis Cardinals, was their pick for the greatest fielder at first base. Through 2011, only nine players owned eleven or more Gold Glove Awards, and among them only Hernandez was a first baseman. He still ranks third for career assists among first basemen, a category he led his league in five times.

Relief pitcher Kent Tekulve called Hernandez

> probably the best glove guy I played against. He was just outstanding with the glove. You couldn't throw a ball by him in the dirt. He handled the ball well. I never saw him give a pitcher a bad feed on a ground ball, no matter if he had to throw it from the hole or if it was a short toss.

As would be expected, Hernandez, many experts' pick as the best fielding first baseman ever, threw lefty, an advantage for the first base position. A right-handed first baseman can't make throws across the diamond, especially on the "first to shortstop back to first" double play, as easily as a portsider, nor can he apply tags on pickoff attempts as deftly and as quickly as a lefty.

Larry Bowa, one of the voters in the 1999 poll, commented, "He made the 3-6-3 double play, a tough play, like no one else ever has." It comes as no surprise then that Hernandez established the record for the most years leading his league in double plays by a first baseman as well as the mark for the most lifetime assists, two true indicators of defensive excellence. In addition, *Sports Illustrated* called him the "best ever at playing the bunt." Hernandez would, on occasion, range far from first base and field bunts on the *third base side* of the infield.

Hernandez was also very aggressive. If, say, a slow grounder was hit to his right and he had to decide in a microsecond whether he should take a chance and go for the more important lead runner at second or take the safe out at first base, he never seemed to make the wrong decision—and his typical brazen move, made unhesitatingly and fearlessly, was to gun the runner out at second, often nailing him by the most narrow of margins.

Although one of Hernandez's managers, Hall of Famer Whitey Herzog, had some problems handling Hernandez, Herzog went even further than many others in his praise, calling Hernandez the best left-handed first baseman that he had ever seen.

Hernandez stressed the fundamentals such as keeping one's glove low to the ground prior to each pitch, charging bunts aggressively, and coming off the bag hard after holding runners on; he was the antithesis of fielders who are lazy, complacent, or unprepared.

WES PARKER
Los Angeles Dodgers 1964–1972

At the 2007 All-Star Game, Rawlings announced the outcome of a promotion they sponsored that began with a list of more than 250 players who owned at least one Gold Glove Award. A panel of experts whittled the group down to 18 outfielders, 5 catchers, 3 pitchers, and 6 men at each infield spot. Finally, a fan election determined the all-time Gold Glove team, commemorating fifty years of Gold Glove Awards. Parker displaced Hernandez at the top spot at first base on the illustrious squad. He commented, "I'm thrilled to be recognized as one of those who worked hard at what is an underappreciated skill."

Unlike the often irrational voting by fans for many spots on All-Star Games, the voting for this defensive team was impeccably done (although most experts saw the Parker selection as a surprise) and featured luminaries such as Willie Mays, Ozzie Smith, Brooks Robinson, Johnny Bench, and Roberto Clemente.

Over his nine-year career with the Los Angeles Dodgers, Parker reeled in six Gold Gloves, all in a row and all of them won during his final years in the majors. In 1965 Parker, who threw left-handed, represented one fourth of baseball's first starting infield made up entirely of switch-hitters. Jim Lefebvre played next to Parker at second base, speedy Maury Wills was at shortstop, and Jim Gilliam manned the hot corner. Parker would end his career with a fielding percentage of .996.

GEORGE SCOTT

Boston Red Sox 1966–1971, 1977–1979; Milwaukee Brewers 1972–1976; Kansas City Royals 1979; New York Yankees 1979

George Scott, who played most of his career for the Red Sox and Brewers, won eight Gold Gloves, the third-best total among first basemen, and he led the AL in assists and in putouts three seasons. His hands would lash out to snare short hops as quickly and as deftly as a frog's tongue striking its prey. Known as Boomer, he led his league in homers and RBI in 1975. His lifetime fielding percentage of .990 revealed him to be a multidimensional player.

Charboneau said that one thing notable about Scott was that "for a big man he moved good." He cited his "footwork around the bag and the way he worked the bag—that comes with experience."

DON MATTINGLY

Yankees legend Mattingly won nine Gold Gloves, trailing only Hernandez among first-sackers. Mattingly, nicknamed Donnie Baseball, had a career fielding percentage that stood at a shimmering .996. In Hernandez's 1994 book, *Pure Baseball*, he selected Mattingly as the best-fielding first baseman of all the men active at that time. His work with the leather was as slick as a con man's patter.

DAVID SEGUI

Baltimore Orioles 1990–1993, 2001–2004; New York Mets 1994–1995; Montreal Expos 1995–1997; Seattle Mariners 1998–1999; Toronto Blue Jays 1999; Texas Rangers 2000; Cleveland Indians 2000

For a time (through the end of the 2000 season) David Segui owned the highest fielding percentage of all first basemen. Veteran pitcher Jesse Orosco called him "the best glove" in the American League, yet few fans recognize just how good he was at first. The son of big league pitcher Diego, David led both the NL (in 1994 with the Mets) and the AL (1992 with the Baltimore Orioles and 1998 with the Seattle Mariners, when he handled 1,162 chances with just one error) in fielding percentage.

━━━━━

Of course, not every player can shine at first base, and certainly not every defensive play around first base is a gem. Some men (for example, see Dick Stuart and Marv Throneberry in chapter 1) earned a lifetime reputation for poor fielding, and others gained a degree of notoriety for a single play.

Two salient examples of botched plays at first, out of a list of many, include costly misplays by Leon Durham and Bill Buckner. In the 1984 NLCS, then a best-of-five playoff, Durham of the Cubs made an error that cost Chicago a late-inning lead and helped the San Diego Padres win the pennant. A sharp grounder went under his glove, through his legs, and into right field despite his cautiously dropping down on a knee to handle the routine play.

Buckner was playing first for the Red Sox when they squared off with the Mets in the 1986 World Series. When Mookie Wilson's slow grounder hugged the line, Buckner took a few strides to get in front of the ball, then, somehow, almost inexplicably, let it get under his mitt. The error permitted the winning run to score and New York went on to top Boston the following day. Take away a gutsy comeback by the Mets, a few other Boston blunders such as a wild pitch that let in the tying run, and Buckner's "E," and the Sox would have clinched their first World Series title since 1918. Through the 1986 season Buckner had four of the five best single season assist totals by a first baseman in baseball history, and once, over a five-year period, he led his league in assists by a first-sacker on four occasions, yet his booted play will be what people remember about him.

4

SOCIALIZING AROUND THE BAG

First basemen handle a position that is conducive to socializing with players from other teams who have reached the bag. There is time to kill between pitches and between batters coming to the plate, and there is proximity between the fielder and the runner he is holding on the bag, so conversation fills the void.

Veteran umpire Fieldin Culbreth said conversations often tend to be of the "How's your family?" nature.

> To be quite honest with you, most of that stuff you'd find to be pretty boring. I guess I would say that it's very much like what would be typical office banter or any other place in the world. It's just that our office happens to be at the corner of first and third.

He pointed out that umpires don't get an awful lot of opportunity to join in discussions with the players and coaches at first and/or third base.

> If you think about it, I'm usually about 10 to 15 feet away and, needless to say, I don't hear most of the conversations and I don't

try to hear most of them. Most of them are typical, "How you doing? What's going on? You been doing all right? How you playing?" Just the typical stuff.

In an interview with Wayne Stewart, Bruce Froemming, one of only two major league umpires to work in over 5,000 contests (Bill Klem was the other), was asked if his conversations around first base were ever interesting. He tersely confirmed what Culbreth had said:

No. Nothing interesting. "How are you? How's your family?" Stuff like that. But it's only said in certain parts [of the game]— it might be early in a game. When the game is on, the only idle conversation we have is if there's a pitching change—you might [talk]. The catcher might say something, but there's nobody out there to socialize.

Culbreth added that

there are some guys [players], just like some umpires, that are more apt to talk to you. Most guys, believe it or not, just don't speak that much. Like I don't do a lot of talking on the field. Most umps don't.

Luis Gonzalez used to be a guy [who] just loved to talk, and he'd come by [as he trotted in or out to his position between innings] and always had something funny to say. To start the game he'd stop and say hello. During the game it might be about one of his at bats. He was fun. Talking with Luis was always entertaining.

One time in Detroit Culbreth saw Gonzalez go

back on a ball, and he was going back, going back, going back. At old Tigers Stadium you could jump up on the fence to elevate yourself [to make a catch]. He ran back as hard as he could, he jumped up on the fence, was prepared to catch the ball, and it hit about 15 feet in front of him. I didn't know it until Luis came back out the next half inning. He stopped and told me, "I just heard one of the funniest things from a fan ever. When I jumped up on the fence and then the ball hit in front of [me], the fan said, 'Hey, nice job, Spider-Man. Instead of climbing the fence, how about just catching the ball?'"

Culbreth concluded that first basemen don't necessarily tend to be chattier than players at other positions. "They just get the opportunity to speak more. Everybody's typically stopped and the coaches are there, so I would say it's just because of the way the game's laid out."

He did concede, though, that Sean Casey stood out as an absolutely

friendly guy, a very friendly guy. I enjoyed seeing and speaking with Sean. It's like I said, though, usually we spoke only when the occasion called for it because the truth is we're out there and everybody's got a job. He's got a job to do—he meaning anybody, not just Sean—and, for the most part, everybody's concentrating on doing their job and I'm doing the same with mine.

Casey, nicknamed the Mayor for his friendly ways, said he got the nickname when he played in the Cape Cod League for Brewster. The holder of a speech communications degree from the University of Richmond recalled that he would arrive at the ballpark

and, you know how I am, I'd be saying hello to everybody. I'd be saying hi to the announcer, hi to the ladies at the gate, and one day [coach Mike] Kirby says to me while I'm coming in, "C'mon, Case. They'll vote for you. They'll vote for you to be mayor."

Casey added that his conversations around the bag are, by and large, mundane, like, "Boy, you sure are hot lately." Nor, said Casey, has he ever spoken to a base runner with the intention of distracting him. If an opponent was a base-stealing threat, the type of man who, at least in part, made his living with his legs, Casey knew to back off. Rickey Henderson was so zoned in that it took Casey an eon to evoke a simple "hi" from the all-time stolen base leader.

On the other hand, over many years Jack Wilson and Casey engaged in discourse at first base from Wilson's rookie season on. Wilson said when he got his first big league hit, in a spring training game, Casey, despite not knowing anything about Wilson, struck up a conversation. Since then they have kept in touch and have even signed bats for each other, inscribing the words "hits and conversation" on them.

Pitcher Nate Robertson, who played for the majority of his career in the American League (which uses the designated hitter rule), has had little occasion to reach first base during his big league days, which began in 2002. Through 2012 he owned just five singles and one double in fifty-four plate appearances. However, he said that the conversation at first base is sometimes "just nonsense. 'Is there a good place to eat in this town?' Tell a joke or two, or they might have some complimentary words to say about a guy's swing that he put on a ball."

Robertson did reveal that players who were close friends or former teammates might exchange insights and "a little more in-depth conversation," including "typically trying to find out what's going on in their life."

Curtis Granderson observed the amount of conversation depends on

if you know him [the first baseman] or not. If it's a guy that you've known or played against or with, the conversation gets a little more in detail. For example, every time I get on with Albert Pujols, our conversation is, "Hey, what's up?" and that's it. I've never said anything more to him; he's never said anything more to me. But guys like Mike Cuddyer with Minnesota or Nick Swisher when he played first base, we had full conversations throughout the entire at bat. I mean constantly—during secondary leads, foul balls, while I'm getting signs, all that different stuff.

It was simply a case of having a different relationship with the latter players. As Granderson pointed out, "I see them a little bit more often."

The range of topics is wide, too, with such players. "It could be, 'Hey, what are you doing in the off season?' 'Where do you live in the off season?' It could be some game stuff that's going on. It's all random."

Aubrey Huff, who was a member of the 2010 and 2012 World Champion San Francisco Giants, said that much of the conversation at first base is "harmless trash talking if you really know the guy well."

Trevor Crowe, an outfielder with the Indians from 2009 through 2011, pointed out an obvious example about the kind of conversation around the bag that is far from inconsequential. "You talk to your first base coach, 'How many outs?' Be aware of the situation and the score of the game."

Granderson said that when he was a rookie things were a bit less social at first base. "I'd still say, 'What's up' to him just because I'm standing there, but their response back [depended on] me knowing them more" as far as whether or not the depth of the conversation increased. Naturally, a rookie does not know as many players as a veteran would.

The convivial Stan Musial was especially kind to rookies. When stationed at first base, any time a player singled for his initial big league hit, Musial would smile and offer him a hearty "Congratulations."

After Chuck Tanner recorded his first hit, Musial greeted him and said, "Nice hitting. You know, I live near you." Tanner said he was taken aback. "Can you imagine that? He said he lives near me, not that I live near him."

Joe Charboneau, former Cleveland Indians outfielder, recalled some friendly first basemen. "Carew took me under his wing, talked hitting with me. He was a good mentor, for lack of a better word. He would even come in and talk to our whole team when we played the Angels." Charboneau joked that on one occasion, when Carew was offering advice, "he was struggling a little bit—I think he was hitting about .350 that year, but he was a fabulous person and player."

Carew even gave informal coaching tips to Charboneau during games when he reached first base.

He'd let you know if you were struggling. He was always willing to help anybody and everybody on their hitting. That's, I think, what was such a great thing when I was in the big leagues— Reggie Jackson would work with me and talk to me—there were a lot of veteran players willing to help you [even] during the game or pre-game. Carew would talk to our hitters before their batting practice. He'd come early. He was really a class act, like most guys in the big leagues were.

However, when Charboneau reached first base

as a rookie, I didn't say much. There was always some small talk, "Look at that girl in the stands. You're having a good year for a rookie. Keep it up. You're swinging the bat [well]." A lot of encouragement.

I remember Clint Hurdle talked to me around the batting cage. "It's been a while since a rookie put up these numbers—keep going." He was really gracious about it.

Today's players pull for one another and do tend to socialize in a very friendly manner.

Kevin Rhomberg stated that was especially true when he'd run across "kids you saw along the [way in the] minor leagues," players who were glad to see that an acquaintance had also made it to the majors.

But what was more interesting as a rookie when you went around was [dealing with] some umpires. They'd all treat you very differently—some were very outgoing and welcoming, "Congratulations. You made it." Another umpire said, "Hey, don't say a word to me, you're a rookie. Just play the game." He wanted to get that established right away; it was really odd. He had that attitude toward players. Most of the guys were cordial, but yet they had a job to do, as the players do, too.

Rhomberg felt that the time and place to socialize should be after the game or "around the cage, because you're out there representing your club, and it could be an old college roommate or an old friend but you still don't express [that chumminess] in front of your teammates during game time."

After a player gains experience in the majors he comes to know more and more players around the league. That's when, according to Charboneau, there would be more interplay beyond just small talk.

I didn't know the guys that well when I first came up, but I would see guys get on first and push and shove each other, tag each other hard, flip their hat or helmet off just to mess around with each other. But it was a little more serious for me because I was in and out of the lineup. I was a rookie. As a rookie, you get on first, pick up your manager right away. They didn't really want a rookie animated like that, doing a lot of that stuff—it was more business for us. I hadn't earned my stripes yet.

In Doug Glanville's book *The Game from Where I Stand*, the former outfielder wrote that he couldn't buy a hit in Atlanta's Turner Field, but one night he singled there off Jason Marquis. He promptly asked for a time-out and requested the ball as a souvenir. Braves first baseman B. J. Surhoff asked the delighted Glanville if he had just reached a career milestone. Glanville replied that there was no special reason for wanting the ball other than that "I finally got a hit here."

Culbreth says that in addition to men such as Musial and Casey, there is definitely a group of first basemen who "tend to talk more than others." That group includes Lance Berkman and Ryan Howard, a self-proclaimed big talker at first. Howard told Bob Costas that he has a topic of the day to discuss with opponents who reach base. Once the "hot topic" concerned why a hitter can be in a groove one day and then, suddenly, finds he can't buy a hit. Howard said the consensus reply to that issue was, "When you find that out, you let me know, 'cause I have no clue." Howard added that he never runs out of things to say, but some of the conversations can't be disclosed to the public.

Froemming said that it was impossible to list just a few of the amiable, conversational players. "There's a whole bunch of guys. You can't pick out one guy." He could, however, go back over his long career and rattle off a ton of friendly players.

And this is being truthful—I could give you twenty guys on every team that were decent guys. And the same two or three that you had trouble with one year, you probably had trouble with every year, because that was their personality and their nature. Better than 90 percent of the guys are decent guys.

When Yogi Berra reached first base he initiated many a conversation, but on the occasions when he saw the hit-and-run sign flashed his way he became subdued, concentrating on his game. Soon opponents noticed the trend and thwarted him by constantly throwing over to keep him anchored near the bag. It wasn't until he countered by learning "to keep up the chatter" that he finally outsmarted the opponents.

A cynic might be suspicious that the players who tend to shoot the breeze with umpires are doing so to become chummy, perhaps hoping an ump will favor them sometime down the road. However, Culbreth, for one, said he never had the impression players were friendly with an ulterior motive in mind.

One of the most unusual, certainly one of the most touching conversations ever to take place around first base occurred moments after Pete Rose lashed a single off Padres pitcher Eric Show on September 11, 1985, to shatter Ty Cobb's long-standing record for the most lifetime hits. After time had been called, Rose's son, Pete Jr., dashed onto the field and greeted his father. The sobbing Rose hugged his son, who later recounted, "Dad being Dad, Mr. Tough Guy, [I'd] never seen him cry before. Never really got a hug or a kiss before. He told me he loved me. I told him I loved him." That emotional moment, Rose Jr. continued, "kind of broke the ice." It was something he would never forget.

Of course, not all social intercourse at first base is friendly. Rhomberg noted how there can be awkwardness, or worse, between, say, a runner and the first baseman just after a baseball donnybrook has been broken up. "It's a little tense sometimes. It all depends on what the issue is. I mean, we [Charleston of Triple-A ball] had some pretty good fights against the Mets organization back in Tidewater, where it got pretty ugly." After one game in which a Charleston player was hit in the head by a pitch, precipitating two bench clearings, one combatant was sent a Godfather-like message. "The clubhouse guy told us there was a dead fish in this certain guy's bag."

Charboneau said he had heard tales about first basemen who made it rough on base-stealing threats, stories about "Lou Brock diving in [back to the bag on pickoff throws], and how they'd tag him hard on the legs."

Take Willie McCovey, a man who was about as strong as they come, and one whom Brock concurred was famous for applying hard tags on runners. McCovey went around 6-foot-4, 200 pounds, and was fittingly called Stretch. He was known to apply a pounding on runners, especially, it seemed, when he wanted to send the message, "You may steal a base on us, but you'll pay a painful cost for doing so." Will Clark was so impressed, he gave a nickname to McCovey's vicious tag, the Sledgehammer.

Others known for their hard tags include Carlos Delgado, Randall Simon, Bill White, and Willie Stargell. Dusty Baker said Stargell would "smile, then drop that hammer on your head, on your ribs. . . . It makes you shorten your lead. The ball would be right in the web of the glove, and it was the ball that hit you on the bone." He added that Stargell "would slap you silly over there, and what could you do?"

Charboneau said that he was fortunate that "nobody ever tagged me hard, nobody ever tried to push me off a bag, nobody ever put a knee in my face," but these things have happened to others. "If I'm sliding back and they did, that's part of the game—it's my fault for coming back headfirst or something. It was a pretty clean game when I played."

And there are other unusual ways for a runner off first base to get hurt or injured. On July 20, 2010, Tampa Bay's speedy Carl Crawford took his lead off first. Well aware that Crawford was a threat to steal, Baltimore pitcher Jake Arrieta threw over to his first baseman, Ty Wigginton. Instead of reaching Arrieta's intended target, his first baseman's mitt, the ball struck Crawford between his legs. He then rolled off the bag and was tagged out. It may have been the type of play that delights viewers of blooper reels or *America's Funniest Videos*, but it wasn't amusing to Crawford, who had to leave the game due to a groin injury.

Charboneau says that Carl Yastrzemski was pretty much all business at first base. "It was about the game. He didn't make a lot of small talk. I saw somebody [a teammate] one time try to give him a high five. He walked by him." The old-school Yaz shunned such celebrations. It was a case of "the new coming in and the old [preferring a traditional handshake over] all the antics and [hand] bumping." Once, when Charboneau stood next to Yaz, he told him how he had been a fan of his as a kid. "He just kind of shook his head. He would just look at you."

From the serious men such as Yaz to the silly ones such as Marvelous Marv, and from the slick fielders to the awesome sluggers, the tales from first base are legion and highly entertaining. What's more, to our delight, they just keep on coming with no end in sight.

ACTION AROUND THE BAG

There have been many memorable plays at or around first base—a few hand-picked ones follow.

Start with the time Cincinnati outfielder Paul O'Neill was playing right field during a 1989 contest. The game rolled into the ninth inning when Steve Jeltz of the Philadelphia Phillies was in scoring position, representing the potential winning run. O'Neill fielded a single cleanly but then, in a hurry to unleash a strong throw to the plate to nail Jeltz and prevent the game from ending, he bobbled the ball several times. Finally, giving up on the play, he angrily kicked the ball, not unlike a football place kicker. Believe it or not, the baseball flew a path straight to Todd Benzinger, the cutoff man at first base, and Jeltz was unable to score.

First base, more than any other position, is the place where controversial and close calls run rampant. Certainly two of the most famous plays at first were the one that may have cost the St. Louis Cardinals the 1985 World Series and another that clearly cost a pitcher a perfect game.

In the sixth game of the 1985 Series St. Louis needed only three outs to clinch the championship when Kansas City's Jorge Orta came to the plate. He hit a high bounder to first baseman Jack Clark, who flipped the ball to Todd Worrell covering first, easily beating Orta to the bag. However, umpire Don Denkinger called the runner safe, triggering a volcanic tirade from the apoplectic Cards. The Royals went on to score twice to win the game and the next day the self-destructing Cardinals, still fuming over the loss, caved, dropping the deciding game, 11–0. They seemed to lose their composure, especially pitcher Joaquin Andujar who was ejected for being way too vociferous over a ball strike call he didn't agree with, a call made by, who else, Denkinger.

Then, more recently, there was an unforgettable play that led to a furor. On June 2, 2010, a blown call on a routine groundout cost Detroit pitcher Armando Galarraga a perfect game. As a matter of fact, it would have been major league baseball's third perfect game over a period of just twenty-five days! With two Cleveland batters out in the ninth inning at the Tigers' Comerica Park, Jason Donald hit a ground ball that was fielded by first baseman Miguel Cabrera, ranging far to his right. His throw to Galarraga, covering first, beat Donald by about a half of a step, but umpire Jim Joyce called him safe.

The next batter, Trevor Crowe, grounded out and the one-hitter, a 3–0 Detroit victory, was completed. After the game, Joyce, clearly distraught as he paced around the umpires' locker room, stated, "It was the biggest call of my career, and I kicked the [stuff] out of it. I just cost that kid a perfect game."

Joyce later met up with Galarraga and, in tears, hugged the pitcher and apologized to him. Galarraga, who had remained, from the moment the call was made and throughout all the controversy, remarkably understanding and forgiving, commented, "You don't see an umpire after the game come out and say, 'Hey, let me tell you I'm sorry.' He felt really bad."

After Galarraga won the game, lifting his record to 2–1 and lowering his ERA on the year to a sparkling 2.57, the Tigers poured onto the field, some to congratulate their pitcher, others to confront and vilify the umpire, well aware that while there was no way to appeal a judgment call, they could still express their disgust.

Galarraga commented that while he was still sad about the situation, "I know that I pitched a perfect game. The first 28-out perfect game." And so, in a way, like Harvey Haddix, who once pitched perfect ball for 12 innings only to have the status of his perfect game stripped by commissioner Fay Vincent in 1991 when he changed the definition of a no-hitter to require a no-hit pitcher to complete the entire game (even extra inning contests) without surrendering a single hit, Galarraga went beyond perfection. That is to say, he went beyond the normal 27 consecutive "outs" without a runner reaching base, yet he received no official accolades for doing so.

With one out in the top of the ninth inning of Game Seven of the wild 1960 World Series, an odd play took place at first base when Rocky Nelson of the Pittsburgh Pirates was holding New York Yankees superstar Mickey Mantle at first as Gil McDougald strolled off third base, taking his lead. With the Pirates up by a 9–8 score, McDougald represented the tying run. Yogi Berra then hit a grounder to Nelson near the bag; Nelson deftly gloved the ball and stepped on first base. He then glanced at second base, preparing to make the throw there to try to consummate a double play. However, Mantle, seeing the force play on him had been wiped out by Nelson's retiring Berra, dove back into first and somehow eluded Nelson, who had, by that point, come to realize the play was right in front of him, and not at second.

Experts later wondered why Nelson simply didn't throw to second immediately to start a 3-to-6-to-3 double play and why Mantle hadn't already bolted toward second with the crack of the bat.

More than a few commended Mantle's quick thinking and nimble feet. Years later on the television series *The Way It Was*, Mantle confessed that he couldn't explain exactly why he dove back to the bag, and he joked that teammate Tony Kubek said it was, in fact, a dumb move.

Pirate center fielder Bill Virdon looked back on the play.

> It looked like a base hit when Berra hit it, and we all were applauding Rocky Nelson for making the play. I think Mantle thought he caught it in the air and was diving back into first and Rocky didn't see him. If he'd have just seen him and tagged him it would have been all over.

Virdon noted Nelson could have either tagged the first base bag, then gone after Mantle, or retired Mantle first and still have concluded the double play at first. "And the run wouldn't have been home yet." Instead the Yanks tied it, setting the stage for Bill Mazeroski to become a World Series legend when he broke the tie in the bottom of the ninth, leading it off with the first ever World Series walk-off home run.

Interestingly, Mantle also disclosed that he tried the same play again the following year, this time against the Boston Red Sox and the man who, in 1960, shared the Pirates' first base duties, Dick Stuart. However, Stuart was not to be duped—he tagged Mantle sharply, allegedly almost fracturing his nose. Stuart then turned to the Yankees slugger and explained, "I was there last year—I saw that [play with Nelson]." It was a case quite similar to the old "Fool me once, shame on you. Fool me twice, shame on me" scenario.

On Independence Day in 1976 Tim McCarver of the Philadelphia Phillies lost a grand slam when he made a huge mistake near first base in a game versus the cross-state Pittsburgh Pirates. Greg Luzinski started off the second inning of the opening game of a doubleheader with a booming triple. Dick Allen coaxed a walk, then Jay Johnstone banged a double to center field that sent Allen sailing into third base. An intentional walk was issued to Garry Maddox to set the stage for McCarver's gaffe. The Phillies catcher hit a towering fly ball to right field. As McCarver followed the flight of the ball, checking to see if it was about to clear the wall or not, he lost sight of the first base bag. Meanwhile, Maddox, too, wondered if the ball would stay in the park and be caught. Because of that possibility, he did not stray far from the bag. At that same time McCarver finally saw that the baseball had cleared the fence, so he began his sprint around the bases. The only problem was, he passed Maddox, who was still fairly close to first base, and by the rules of the game, McCarver was declared out. That reduced his "home run" to a mere single, which he had earned the moment he touched first base. He cost his team a run but the Phillies, behind ace Steve Carlton, went on to win a 10–5 laugher.

Another odd play around first base occurred during the fourth game of the 1978 World Series between the New York Yankees and the Los Angeles Dodgers. Los Angeles led by a 3–1 score in the sixth inning, but New York had Reggie Jackson on first and team captain Thurman Munson on second, with Lou Piniella at the plate. Piniella hit what seemed to be an easy ball to turn for a double play. Shortstop Bill Russell gobbled the ball up, stepped on the second base bag, then fired to first.

That's when Jackson decided the only way to avoid a twin killing was to stick his right hip into the path of the baseball. Sure enough, the ball struck him and bounded away. Piniella was safe at first and the inning, which seemed to be headed for futility, continued. Somehow the umpires felt Jackson's movement was not intended to interfere with the play and that judgment call stood despite vitriolic protests from the Dodgers.

The examples could go on and on, but let's end with a moment of levity. Way back in 1911 Herman "Germany" Schaefer of the Washington Senators was on first base and teammate Clyde Milan was on third. Schaefer decided that if he lit off for second he would draw a throw from the catcher, which would give Milan the opportunity to steal home, but the catcher decided he would not make the throw and Schaefer slid into second unchallenged. Not to be thwarted or out-smarted, he decided he'd set up that same play once more, but to do so he'd have to return to first base! After his crazy burst of inspiration, he pulled off a "steal" of first base, with the catcher again making no throw. Legend has it that (a) on the very next pitch Schaefer was running and, once more, stole second base, and (b) Milan was successful in swiping home amid all the chaos of one of baseball's wildest plays ever.

APPENDIX
FIRST BASEMEN IN THE HALL OF FAME

Through the 2011 induction ceremony at the National Baseball Hall of Fame, twenty-five first basemen have been honored in Cooperstown, according to a list of Hall of Famers and their positions posted at the Hall's website, http://baseballhall.org/hall-famers/members/searchable-data.

A handful of these men are not covered in this book, since it focuses on men who played their entire careers in the major leagues after 1900 (Frank Chance, 1898–1914, is the only exception). George Kelly (1915–1932), who didn't seem to fit in any of the book's chapters, is the only modern-era Hall of Famer who was excluded from these pages. Four of the following men were Negro League stars: the legendary Buck Leonard; Oscar Charleston, a center fielder who some claim was the greatest, most well-rounded Negro League player ever and whose fielding rivaled that of Tris Speaker (this standout moved to first base late in his career); Mule Suttles, a tape measure home run artist; and Ben Taylor.

Here, then, are the Hall of Fame first basemen:

- Cap Anson
- Ernie Banks
- Jake Beckley
- Jim Bottomley
- Dan Brouthers
- Rod Carew

- Orlando Cepeda
- Frank Chance
- Oscar Charleston
- Roger Connor
- Jimmie Foxx
- Lou Gehrig
- Hank Greenberg
- George Kelly
- Harmon Killebrew
- Buck Leonard
- Willie McCovey
- Johnny Mize
- Eddie Murray
- Stan Musial
- Tony Perez
- George Sisler
- Mule Suttles
- Ben Taylor
- Bill Terry

BIBLIOGRAPHY

Books

Adomites, Paul, Bobby Cassidy, and Saul Wisnia. *Sluggers! History's Heaviest Hitters.* Lincolnwood, IL: Publications International, Ltd., 1999.

Bouton, Jim. *Ball Four.* New York: Dell Publishing, 1970.

Dickson, Paul. *Baseball's Greatest Quotations.* New York: HarperResource, 1992.

Glanville, Doug. *The Game from Where I Stand: A Ballplayer's Inside View.* New York: Times Books, 2010.

Golenbock, Peter. *Wrigleyville: A Magical History Tour of the Chicago Cubs.* New York: St. Martin's, 1996.

Green, Lee. *Sportswit: All the Clever Rejoinders, Wry Observations, Classic Tales, Poignant Phrases, Apt One-Liners, and Inane Comments From and About the World of Sports.* New York: HarperCollins, 1984.

Hernandez, Keith, and Mike Bryan. *Pure Baseball: Pitch by Pitch for the Advanced Fan.* New York: HarperCollins Children's, 1994.

Johnson, Lloyd. *Baseball's Book of Firsts.* Philadelphia: Running Press, 1999.

Kerrane, Kevin, ed. *"Batting Cleanup, Bill Conlin."* Philadelphia: Temple University Press, 1997.

Leventhal, Josh, ed. *Baseball and the Meaning of Life.* Minneapolis: Voyageur Press, 2005.

Nathan, David H., ed. *Baseball Quotations: The Wisdom and Firecracks of Players, Managers, Owners, Umpires, Announcers, Writers, and Fans on the Greatest American Pastime*. New York: Ballantine Books, 1993.

The Sporting News *Selects Baseball's 100 Greatest Players: A Celebration of the 20th Century's Best*. St. Louis, MO: Sporting News Publishing Company, 1999.

Stewart, Wayne. *Baseball Oddities: Bizarre Plays and Other Funny Stuff*. New York: Sterling, 1998.

———. *Fathers, Sons, and Baseball: Our National Pastimes and the Ties That Bond*. Guilford, CT: Lyons Press, 2002.

———. *Hitting Secrets of the Pros: Big League Sluggers Reveal the Tricks of Their Trade*. New York: McGraw-Hill, 2004.

———. *Stan the Man: The Life and Times of Stan Musial*. Chicago: Triumph Books, 2010.

Turbow, Jason, with Michael Duca. *The Baseball Codes: Beanballs, Sign Stealing, and Bench-Clearing Brawls: The Unwritten Rules of America's Pastime*. New York: Pantheon, 2010.

Magazines

Andriesen, David. "Mariners Relate Each Position's Toughest Plays." *Baseball Digest* (December 2003): 42.

Callahan, Tom. "A Rose Is a Rose Is a Rose." *Time* (August 19, 1985).

Center, Bill. "Andres Galarraga Swings for the Fences." *Baseball Digest* (July 2000): 72.

"Detroit Tigers." *USA Today Sports Weekly* (April 13–19, 2011): 15.

Elderkin, Phil. "Eddie Murray Defies the Sophomore Jinx." *Baseball Digest* (September 1978): 49.

Feeney, Charley. "Switch to First Base Angers Bucs' Oliver." *Sporting News* (May 11, 1974): 8.

Kurkjian, Tim. "Good Hands People." *Sports Illustrated* (1996 special issue): 54.

Minshew, Wayne. "Mom's Tips Put Evans on Track." *Sporting News* (June 1, 1974).

Rains, Rob. "Kruk's Gut Reaction: Avoid All Scales." *USA Today Baseball Weekly* (February 23–March 1, 1994).

Reilly, Rick. "The Big Heart." *Sports Illustrated* (August 8, 1994): 18–19, 22.

Ryan, Bob. "1967 Carl Yastrzemski Wins A.L. Triple Crown." *Baseball Digest* (November 2000): 70.

Starr, Mark. "High and Inside; It was Hardly a Surprise to Learn that One of Baseball's Biggest Stars Had Used Steroids. That's Part of the Problem. (Jason Giambi)." *Newsweek* (December 2004).

Strauss, Joe. "Baseball's Best Player Albert Pujols." *Baseball Digest* (August 2009): 22.

Verducci, Tom. "Bay Area Bombers." *Sports Illustrated* (July 17, 2000).

Wendel, Tim. "No Time for Talk." *USA Today Baseball Weekly* (June 21–27, 1995).

White, Paul. "Big Sticks." *USA Today Sports Weekly* (August 9–15, 2006): 10.

——. "Defensive Players Who Measure Up." *USA Today Sports Weekly* (April 21–27, 2010): 24.

Newspapers

Ahrens, Frank. "Left-Handed Praise in Mainstream World; Why Lefties Just Look Better Swinging a Bat." *Washington Post*, October 27, 1999.

Andriesen, David. "Sosa Steals the Show Giambi Wins Competition, Cubs Slugger Inspires Awe." *Seattle Post-Intelligencer*, July 9, 2002.

Blum, Ronald. "Giambi Will Meet with Mitchell 'Personal History' of Steroids Use." *Cincinnati (OH) Post*, June 22, 2007.

——. "Steroids testimony may open Giambi to punishment." *Charleston (WV) Gazette*, December 3, 2004.Boswell, Thomas. "A Pair of Ones-of-a-Kind Upgrade the Hall Today; Yastrzemski, Bench: Work Ethic, Talent." *Washington Post*, July 23, 1989.

Couch, Greg. "Stranded at Gates of Hall Canseco, McGriff Might Have Jeopardized Chances with Uneven Performances Late in their Careers." *Chicago Sun-Times*, May 16, 2002.

Dicker, Ron. "Catchers Who Hit Honor One of Their Own." *New York Times*, June 19, 2004.

Fallstrom, R. B. "BBN—Reds-Cardinals." AP Online. 1998.

Feldman, Bruce. "The Coolest Carlos Delgado Cleans Up Nicely On and Off The Field." *Chicago Sun-Times*. 2001.

Gregor, Scot. "Paul Konerko Superstar? It May Happen Soon." *Daily Herald* (Arlington Heights, IL), March 5, 2000.

Hertzel, Bob. "Living Legend." *Pittsburgh Press*, April 19, 1985.

Horrigan, Jeff. "Red Sox Notebook; Williamson set to get active." *Boston Herald*, September 8, 2004.

Hoynes, Paul. "Detroit's Cabrera Scares the Daylights out of Acta." *Plain Dealer* (OH), May 2, 2011.

Kiley, Mike. "A Change of Grace: Clean Living Already Paying Dividends." *Chicago Sun-Times*, February 24, 1999.

——. "Grace Gets the Dirt on Rockies' Walker." *Chicago Sun-Times*, July 28, 1997.

Kinney, Terry. "Marge's Mess Embattled Reds' Owner Unlikely to Give up Ownership of Her Club." *Albany (NY) Times Union*, December 6, 1992.

McCoy, Hal. "Concepcion Gets Emotional as Reds Retire No. 13 Former Reds Shortstop, was All-Star, Gold Glove Winner and Sliver Slugger Award Winner." *Dayton (OH) Daily News*, August 26, 2007.

———. "Reds to Honor Senior." *Dayton (OH) Daily News*, February 13, 2004.

McDonough, Will. "Hallmark of Fame Yastrzemski Gets a Hero's Reception at Cooperstown." *Boston Globe*, July 24, 1989.

"Met Life: Delgado Swings with Gusto; Snaps Power Drought with Two Homers, Five RBI to Help Maine Collect sixth victory." *Chicago Sun-Times*, May 27, 2007.

"Rays' Crawford Leaves Game." *Chronicle-Telegram* (Elyria, OH), July 21, 2010.

Salisbury, Jim. "Players such as McGriff May Find Hall of Fame Chance Enhanced Because of Steroids." *Philadelphia Inquirer*, March 13, 2004.

Staff Reports. "Reds, Dodgers to Meet in Vegas; The March 31 Exhibition Game will be Cincinnati's First Time Playing in the Vacation Hot Spot." *Dayton (OH) Daily News*, January 26, 2010.

Walker, Ben. "Pair Set for Hall." *Chronicle-Telegram* (Elyria, OH), January 6, 2011.

Websites

Baseball Almanac, www.baseball-almanac.com
The Baseball Page, www.thebaseballpage.com
Baseball Reference, www.baseballreference.com
Jock Bio, www.jockbio.com

Interviews

Howard, Ryan, interviewed by Bob Costas from *Studio 42 with Bob Costas*, an MLB production.

The following interviews were conducted by Wayne Stewart:

Aaron, Hank (baseball player), phone interview, November 2009.
Bagwell, Jeff (baseball player), Cincinnati, OH, August 2003, and Houston, TX, July 2001.
Blyleven, Bert (baseball player), Baltimore, MD, c. August 1992.
Bosman, Dick (baseball player), Baltimore, MD, c. August 1992.
Carter, Joe (baseball player), Toronto, ONT, c. July 1993.
Charboneau, Joe (baseball player), Lorain, OH, August 2011.
Crowe, Trevor (baseball player), Cleveland, OH, September 2009.
Culbreth, Fieldin (major league umpire), phone interview, August 2009.
Dawson, Andre (baseball player), Toronto, ONT, c. July 1993.

Dempsey, Rick (baseball player), Baltimore, MD, c. August 1992.

Erstad, Darin (baseball player), Cleveland, OH, September 2004.

Face, Elroy (baseball player), phone interview, June 2008.

Froemming, Bruce (major league umpire), phone interview, September 2009.

Grace, Mark (baseball player), Detroit, MI, June 2003.

Granderson, Curtis (baseball player), Cleveland, OH, September 2009.

Groat, Dick (baseball player), phone interview, July 2008.

Harwell, Ernie (Detroit Tigers broadcaster), Detroit, MI, June 2003, and Detroit, MI, July 2000.

Helton, Todd (baseball player), Pittsburgh, PA, August 2003.

Huff, Aubrey (baseball player), Cleveland, OH, September 2009.

Jarvis, Andy (baseball player and manager), Lorain, OH, c. July 2009.

Jefferies, Gregg (baseball player), Detroit, MI, July 2000.

Koplove, Mike (baseball player), Detroit, MI, June 2003.

LaRoche, Adam (baseball player), Philadelphia, PA, August 2004.

Olerud, John E. (baseball player), Cleveland, OH, c. June 2001.

Olerud, John G. (baseball player), Cleveland, OH, June 2005.

Orosco, Jesse (baseball player), Cleveland, OH, c. August 1998.

Robertson, Nate (baseball player), Cleveland, OH, September 2009.

Shuba, George (baseball player), phone interview, April 2008.

Spiezio, Ed (baseball player), phone interview, June 2001.

Tekulve, Kent (baseball player), Cincinnati, OH, August 2003.

Tettleton, Mickey (baseball player), Cleveland, OH, c. July 1993.

Westlake, Wally (baseball player), phone interview, July 2008.

Zabransky, Charles (New York Yankees clubhouse worker), phone interview, c. July 2006.

INDEX

ABOUT THE AUTHORS

Wayne Stewart was born and raised in Donora, Pennsylvania, a town that has produced several big league baseball players, including Stan Musial and the father-son Griffeys. In fact, he was a member of the same Donora High School baseball team as Griffey Sr. Stewart, who retired from teaching after thirty-one years, now lives in Amherst, a suburb of Cleveland, Ohio.

Stewart began covering the sports world as a writer in 1978, freelancing for publications such as *Baseball Digest, Beckett Baseball Card Monthly, Baseball Bulletin*, and *Boys' Life*, and for official team publications of ten major league clubs. He has interviewed and profiled many stars, including Larry Bird, Nolan Ryan, Bob Gibson, Rickey Henderson, and Ken Griffey Jr., and has written biographies of Babe Ruth, Stan Musial, and Alex Rodriguez. Stewart is also a prolific writer; among his twenty-nine books are *Baseball Oddities; Fathers, Sons, and Baseball;* and *You're the Umpire.*

As a baseball expert and historian, Stewart has also appeared on numerous radio and television shows, including an episode about Bob Feller on ESPN's *SportsCentury* Classic program on Bob Feller. He also hosted several radio shows for a Lorain, Ohio, station, including pre-game reports prior to Notre Dame football games and Cleveland Indians baseball games, as well as a call-in talk show.

Brad Engel was born in Evanston, Illinois, and raised in Chicago's northwest suburb of Hanover Park, which does not have a Musial to its name, but instead a Sal Fasano and an Alan Levine. Brad now lives in Roselle, Illinois.

Engel has covered sports professionally since 1999. He met coauthor Stewart on Cal Ripken Jr. weekend at the new Comiskey Park in 2001. Since becoming a journalist, Engel has served as a sports reporter and sports editor for media outlets currently owned by AOL, Lee Enterprises, and Sun-Times Media. He has also freelanced for a national print media publication (*90:00 Soccer* magazine) and multiple major metro newspapers, including coverage of Notre Dame's football team for the *Chicago Sun-Times*.

Engel has covered a Super Bowl, a PGA Championship, an MLS Cup, and both men's and women's NCAA Final Fours. He has won five national writing awards and the Chicago Headline Club's Peter Lisagor Award.

Engel's memorable one-on-one interviews include those with Jackie Joyner-Kersee, Pat Summitt, Candace Parker, Jeanette "the Black Widow" Lee, and Brian Urlacher.

This is Engel's first book.